WHAT PEOPLE ARE SAYING ABOUT
TRACY STRAWBERRY AND *THE COURAGE TO HEAL...*

In *The Courage to Heal*, Tracy Strawberry writes about the hard things people go through, including guilt, shame, regret, consequences of the past, and feelings of being trapped in a cycle of failure, dysfunction, or defeat. Tracy does so with empathy, encouragement, and grace. At the same time, she demonstrates the saving, healing, and redeeming power of God through her own life story, the power of the Holy Spirit, practical application, and godly principles. No matter what area of life you struggle with, you will find true encouragement and a clear pathway forward.

—*Joni Lamb*
Founder, Daystar Television Network

In *The Courage to Heal*, Tracy Strawberry is very transparent about her difficult life as well as her deep struggle to surrender her life to Jesus Christ. She shares openly about how her hurts and rebellion created a damaging, self-destructive belief system about God through her own opinions, worldly desires, and past experiences. She fought God with every fiber of her being until desperation and losing custody of her three sons brought her to her knees and led her to find the courage to heal. She opened her heart to dare to believe—and receive—the purity and power of God's truth and love, which completely healed and transformed her into the mighty woman of God she is today.

—*Jack Graham*
Pastor, Prestonwood Baptist Church, Plano, TX
PowerPoint Ministries

In *The Courage to Heal*, Tracy Strawberry shows how to get on the pathway to freedom from addictions and dysfunctional patterns of loving and living that keep us bound, stuck, broken, and hopeless. As you apply the direction and godly principles Tracy delivers in this powerful book, you will find yourself experiencing freedom through the power of God and the process of change. Tracy leads you in a no-nonsense, step-by-step process with encouragement, love, and belief in you!

—*Real Talk Kim*
Pastor, international speaker, author, CEO, and creator

We all need someone in our lives who believes in a hopeful future for us, no matter what we might be going through, what we have done in our past, or what might have been done to us. As you read the pages of *The Courage to Heal: Moving Beyond Your Habits, Your Past, and Your Pain*, Tracy Strawberry becomes that hopeful and encouraging voice in your life. She has overcome dysfunctional loving and living, severe addiction, deep heartache, betrayal, and regret, to name a few. In her book, Tracy takes you step-by-step on a powerful journey of healing and wholeness! She provides a strong hand to lift you up from wherever you have fallen—or may have gotten stuck in life—by giving you proven, practical solutions and encouragement along the way. Tracy is someone who truly understands where you are now and shows you how to become everything you were meant to be.

—*Ron and Hope Carpenter*
Founders and Pastors, Redemption church, Greenville, SC
Speakers and authors, *The Necessity of an Enemy* and
The Most Beautiful Disaster

Tracy Strawberry has been a dear personal friend of mine for over fifteen years. I have watched her be a witness and a help to multitudes, walking people through a life-transforming, healing journey with Jesus Christ and a proven pathway of change. The impact I have personally observed in people's lives, time after time, is true, lasting change. The information in her new book, *The Courage to Heal*, has been in high demand for years and is finally in printed form and available to anyone seeking deep healing or desiring to overcome obstacles or life issues that keep them bound to defeat. Tracy understands, from a deep personal place, the journey of healing and how to break through some of the greatest of strongholds, including addictions, alcoholism, betrayal, unhealthy relationships, and dysfunctional life patterns. Every page is filled with promise and power. Get your copy today and begin your healing journey!

—Joanne Hoehne
Lead Pastor, The Source Church, Bradenton, FL
Author, speaker, and trainer of pastors

We have known Tracy Strawberry for over ten years. She has an amazing heart to help people and see them set free and healed. As you read *The Courage to Heal*, you will feel like it was written just for you! You might be facing a broken relationship, struggling under the grip of addiction, suffering from emotional trauma, or dealing with some other debilitating situation. What you need is real healing. To get started on that process, you require a strong boost of courage and the will to persevere. Tracy Strawberry draws on her years of experience in helping thousands of other people move into a new life as she guides you to that place of healing. Tracy effectively weaves in the story of her own past issues and breakthroughs as she describes the series of powerful choices we can all make to become whole again.

—Chris Luppo
TV producer/manager and speaker
—John Luppo
Entrepreneur, evangelist, and speaker, Luppo Ministries

In *The Courage to Heal*, Tracy Strawberry provides a powerful resource. She documents her own real-life tragedies, life-controlling issues, addictions, brokenness, guilt, shame, and regret. But that is not all! She also beautifully and dynamically details the pathway to healing, triumph, freedom, power, and purpose! We have had the absolute privilege of pastoring Darryl and Tracy and knowing them personally for several years now. Pastor Tracy is fully devoted to leading people into the same life-saving, healing, and transforming power of Christ she has so wonderfully experienced. She will, without a doubt, challenge, encourage, and guide you through biblical principles to receive God's healing power and the breakthrough you deserve.

—*Jesse and Missy Quiroz*
Lead Pastors, Journey Church, Troy, MO

It's easy to want a "magic formula" that will solve all our problems. But by courageously working through our issues one choice at a time, we gain new strength, and we suddenly find ourselves growing into the freedom we seek. In *The Courage to Heal*, Tracy Strawberry shows how to break free from addictions and dysfunctional patterns that keep us bound, stuck, broken, and hopeless. She keeps it real and delivers the powerful truth of God's Word that can heal any heart and break any chain that binds! As you apply the principles in this book, you will begin to experience the transforming and healing power of God through His great love and unfailing faithfulness!

—*Pastor Kevin McGuinness*
Jesus Is Lord Church, Holtsville, NY

In *The Courage to Heal*, Tracy Strawberry defines trust, forgiveness, healing, and boundaries in a brilliant way, illuminating the shadowy corners of deception in the soul. Through easy-to-understand, practical principles, this book empowers you to overcome whatever difficulties you are facing and leads you right into the flowing love and power of God. If you want to be healed and free, this book is a must-read!

—*Brenda Crouch*
Author, speaker, and television host

THE COURAGE TO HEAL

MOVING BEYOND YOUR HABITS, YOUR PAST, AND YOUR PAIN

TRACY STRAWBERRY

WHITAKER
HOUSE

Note: This book is not intended to provide medical or psychological advice or to take the place of medical advice and treatment from your personal physician. Those who are having suicidal thoughts or who have been emotionally, physically, or sexually abused should seek help from a mental health professional or qualified counselor. Neither the publisher nor the author nor the author's ministry takes any responsibility for any possible consequences from any action taken by any person reading or following the information in this book. If readers are taking prescription medications, they should consult with their physicians and not take themselves off prescribed medicines without the proper supervision of a physician. Always consult your physician or other qualified health care professional before undertaking any change in your physical regimen, whether fasting, diet, medications, or exercise.

Scripture quotations marked (MSG) are taken from *The Message: The Bible in Contemporary Language* by Eugene H. Peterson, © 1993, 1994, 1995, 1996, 2000, 2001, 2002, 2018. Used by permission of NavPress Publishing Group. All rights reserved. Represented by Tyndale House Publishers, Inc. Scripture quotations marked (AMP) are taken from *The Amplified® Bible*, © 2015 by The Lockman Foundation, La Habra, CA. Used by permission. (www.Lockman.org). All rights reserved. Scripture quotations marked (AMPC) are taken from *The Amplified® Bible, Classic Edition*, © 1954, 1958, 1962, 1964, 1965, 1987 by The Lockman Foundation. Used by permission (www.Lockman.org). All rights reserved. Scripture quotations marked (NLT) are taken from the *Holy Bible, New Living Translation*, © 1996, 2004, 2015 by Tyndale House Foundation. Used by permission of Tyndale House Publishers, Inc., Carol Stream, Illinois 60188. All rights reserved. Scripture quotations marked (ESV) are taken from *The Holy Bible, English Standard Version*, © 2000, 2001, 1995 by Crossway Bibles, a division of Good News Publishers. Used by permission. All rights reserved. Scripture quotations marked (NIV) are taken from the *Holy Bible, New International Version®*, NIV®, © 1973, 1978, 1984, 2011 by Biblica, Inc.® Used by permission. All rights reserved worldwide. The "NIV" and "New International Version" are trademarks registered in the United States Patent and Trademark Office by Biblica, Inc.® Scripture quotations marked (KJV) are taken from the King James Version of the Holy Bible. All rights reserved. Scripture quotations marked (NKJV) are taken from the *New King James Version*, © 1979, 1980, 1982 by Thomas Nelson, Inc. Used by permission. All rights reserved. Scripture quotations marked (HCSB) are taken from *The Christian Standard Bible*, © 2017 by Holman Bible Publishers. Used by permission. Christian Standard Bible®, and CSB® are federally registered trademarks of Holman Bible Publishers. All rights reserved.

The forms LORD and GOD (in small capital letters) in Bible quotations represent the Hebrew name for God *Yahweh* (Jehovah), while *Lord* and *God* normally represent the name *Adonai*, in accordance with the Bible version used.

THE COURAGE TO HEAL:
Overcoming Your Habits, Your Past, and Your Pain

www.TracyStrawberry.com

ISBN: 978-1-64123-901-1 • eBook ISBN: 978-1-64123-902-8
© 2022 by Tracy Strawberry
Printed in Colombia

Whitaker House • 1030 Hunt Valley Circle • New Kensington, PA 15068
www.whitakerhouse.com

LC record available at https://lccn.loc.gov/2022021581
LC ebook record available at https://lccn.loc.gov/2022021582

1 2 3 4 5 6 7 8 9 10 11 ⊔⊔ 29 28 27 26 25 24 23 22

CONTENTS

FOREWORD

We all have struggles in life. We might be stuck in fear, anger, doubt, addiction, dysfunctional patterns, codependency, or other entrenched habits that continually hold us back from fulfillment and success. A lot of people are afraid to talk about their struggles. They may feel like their situations are so overwhelming that they don't know where to begin to turn things around. Many don't trust themselves to be able to change.

I fully understand what that is like. I felt that way for many years. But I also discovered this: you can never get well if you don't talk about your struggles and learn how to make positive choices that lead to transformation. The turning point often comes when someone or something unexpected comes into your life and shows you that there's hope—that there's a different way of doing things than the way you've been doing them. That you don't have to live in defeat anymore. That you can become free of what has been holding that hard grip on your life. That you can have the courage to heal from the pain of the wrong choices you have made, the hurts you have inflicted, and the hurts others have imposed on you.

That unexpected event happened to me when I met my wife, Tracy. I was at the lowest point of my life, slowly dying from my addictions and other destructive patterns. I was completely broken and separated from God and lost in a dysfunctional lifestyle. But, in Tracy, I saw someone who was committed to God and to the process of change. What was really dear to my heart at the beginning of our relationship was that she was constantly living out God's ways, no matter what the circumstances looked like—whether they were good, bad, or indifferent. And what she was doing was *working*. She was turning her life around through her close relationship with God, her renewed outlook, and her courageous choices. She had discovered biblical truths and practical principles for overcoming a host of issues she had battled since she was a child. What she had learned and put into practice was changing her life, one choice at a time.

I'm a much better man today because Tracy is in my life. I would never have been able to get to the place of healing and breakthrough where I am now—in fact, I might not even be alive right now—if it hadn't been for her and the power of God working through her life. I was completely broken and separated from God, lost in a dysfunctional lifestyle, living in a way that was the total opposite of a godly life. But as I saw Tracy consistently living out life-changing principles, as I saw her enduring disappointments and trials with grace, and as I witnessed the powerful results in her life, I wanted what she had. I wanted the same courage to heal from the pain in my life.

That's when God challenged me with this thought: "If you want what she has, you're going to have to do what she's doing."

Tracy's faith and determination to turn her life around have always been a great inspiration to me and helped me to follow the same path to victory. But I had to take the principles and actively apply them to my own life. I had to do the necessary work. I had to be consistent. I had to persevere. She showed the way, but I needed to do my part. In *The Courage to Heal*, she shows you the way and invites you to take those powerful steps too.

Through Tracy, I also learned who God truly is. Previously, I had talked about God, but I had no real relationship with Him or knowledge about what He was like. Tracy put her relationship with God first. I was in awe that someone could really live in joy and strength every day, even when things were not going well. That attracted my attention and made me realize I needed to do something different if I wanted to know God myself. I had to surrender to God, study His Word, and spend time with the Lord to develop an ongoing relationship with Him.

We can spend our lives sitting in the realm of "If only I had…" "I should have…" and "I could have…." Or, we can get up and say, "I'm going to press forward, and I'm not going to look to the left or to the right or behind me. I'm going to keep moving ahead, because I know God's got something good for me."

Let me tell you: God has something good for you! You can learn to be an overcomer, no matter what issues you're struggling with, in the same way Tracy learned to be an overcomer, and in the same way I learned to be overcomer by following her example and the powerful principles for change she applied and illustrated by her life. Whether you're dealing with emotional pain, negative habits, difficult relationships, or addictions, you can live in the fullness of God's purpose for your life as you eliminate the obstacles that are hindering you.

You can do this only by God's transforming power and a determination to change the patterns that have led to frustration, pain, despair, and defeat. Because Tracy has bravely gone through the process of change, she is able to guide you in rebuilding your life from the ground up and then flourishing in wholeness of spirit, mind, and body. In this book, she shows you how to have victory over your past, reinvent yourself, move forward, and become the very best "you" the Lord created you to be.

The Courage to Heal is not just about removing hindrances from our lives. It is also about becoming free so we can live with purpose, significance, and joy, just as God intended, realizing the potential and gifts He's placed within us. That's something else that Tracy has continually demonstrated to me. Even while she continued to heal from her hurts and dysfunctions, she began to enter into her full potential in life. She resurrected her dreams and goals and accomplished even more than she ever imagined she would—going back to school and earning her doctorate, starting businesses, and ministering her message of hope and healing around the world.

None of that happened overnight. It took perseverance. It took taking steps outside of her comfort zone and saying, "God, I trust You, and I believe I can do these things in You." This was all part of her process of growth and change as she maintained a lifestyle of discovering and applying godly, practical principles to her everyday life. I'm continually impressed by all the things she overcomes and achieves because she puts herself and her own personal feelings aside to allow God to be in charge of her life. She yields herself to Him so His power can work through her.

Tracy has received grace and power from God, but she hasn't kept them to herself. What I love most about my wife is the love and care she has for other people. In our marriage, God has enabled us to minister together, extending hope and healing to many family members, couples, individuals, young people, and others. But I had to go through a process to understand what it means to help others with the help I had received. Let me give you one example.

After we were first married, Tracy regularly hosted a group of young people at our home. She called it "Friday Night Freedom." I would come back from a road trip, and I'd see all these kids sitting around our living room with their feet up on the furniture, just hanging out, and I would think, "What in the world is this? Go on home!" But I soon realized that God had called Tracy to pour into these young people's lives and have a godly impact on them, helping them with both spiritual and practical needs. Some of those kids were runaways or were dealing with other distressing situations in their lives. They all called my wife "Mama Tracy." She was filling in what was missing from their broken lives. Our house became a home of hope and healing. So, initially, when I internally protested about those kids being there, God said to me, "Shhh. Don't you say anything! You stay quiet."

God had redeemed Tracy's life, and now He was using her to minister to a generation of young people who were suffering. And He has used her in numerous other ways to minister to many people through the years. Once God heals you, enabling you to move beyond your habits, your past, and your pain, your life will be used to bring healing to others as well. That's His plan of hope and restoration for us all.

If I hadn't met Tracy, I don't know where I would be today. I might not be sold out for Christ or an evangelist preaching the gospel. She showed me what it means to make right choices and then *keep on* making right choices regardless of the circumstances. Having the courage to heal is about not giving up. Many people give up before the miracle takes place.

We all want the miracle, but we don't want to do the work. Tracy has done the work—and because she has done that work, she is able to point the way, by proven experience, to lasting healing and an abundant life in Christ. Healing that leads to true change comes by making difficult but positive choices, trusting in God, taking practical steps, staying the course, and fighting for the freedom you deserve.

I love Tracy deeply, and I am so proud that she did not allow her pain, addictions, and dysfunctional loving and living to define her but instead recognized they were obstacles she was in the process of overcoming. In *The Courage to Heal*, Tracy presents step-by-step solutions based on her own life transformation and over twenty years of helping others to achieve the same through the power of God and the process of change. She guides you into a fresh start, new hope, and lasting change! In this book, as in her life, her encouragement is contagious.

I'm blessed to have Tracy in my life every day. And it's a joy to me that, through this book, you can have Tracy in your life too—encouraging you, showing you God's love, and assuring you that you can start today to find genuine healing and a brand-new life.

—*Darryl Strawberry*

ACKNOWLEDGMENTS

To my Lord and Savior, Jesus Christ! There are no words that could give You all the honor and praise that You alone deserve! There is none like You! To God, our Father, be all the glory!

To my incredible husband, for your unconditional love and support. You are the most powerful man of God I know, and the most amazing husband and father to our entire family. I love you beyond words! You have fought tremendous battles in the public eye and behind closed doors, and you have come through victoriously. Your strength has always inspired me. You are the love of my life, forever and always.

To my sons, Omar, Austin, and Evan: you are the real heroes. You are amazing men who have fought to create the successful lives you have today. I'm so proud of each one of you. We were once separated and lost, but now we are found and filled with a great love that nothing or no one can separate. I love you from the depths of my soul, and I'm so grateful you opened your hearts to me once again.

To our children, Omar, Austin, Evan, Alice, Jordan, Jade, Jewel, Diamond, and D.J.: your path has not been easy, and I am astounded by your tremendous strength and perseverance. You have become amazing men and women. I love you all so very much. I thank you for opening your hearts to me and allowing us all to heal and become one as a family.

To my father, Gerry, and my mother, Peggy: your unconditional love, in which I was raised, never left me. It drew me back home and out of my darkness. You are the most amazing parents a child could ask for. I'm beyond grateful for you, for the way you raised me, for every sacrifice you ever made for me, and for the deep love you have always had for me. I love and cherish you both beyond words.

To my sisters, Lisa, Tammy, and Angie, who never gave up on me and have loved me right into my healing. I love you so very much!

To Lee Weeks, who helped me through the creative process of writing this book. I am grateful for your strength, your creative abilities, and the encouragement you always gave that got me through this journey.

To Christine, Lois, and the Whitaker House team: you are every bit of amazing! Thank you for believing in me and God's work through me, and for giving me your very best!

INTRODUCTION:
THE PATHWAY TO HEALING

Have you ever said—or thought—any of these reflections, despairing because you felt a new beginning or a healed heart was impossible for you?

+ "I can't seem to let go of my past."

+ "Will love ever work out for me?"

+ "I'm overwhelmed by sadness and depression."

+ "I can't forgive myself or those who have hurt me."

+ "I just want to break free!"

+ "God, where are You?"

+ "How long is this going to last?"

+ "Can I truly begin again and move forward in life?"

I have expressed every one of those comments. My addiction to drugs and alcohol, dysfunctional relationships, betrayals, bitterness, brokenness, and bad choices took me farther than I ever wanted to go and kept me there longer than I ever wanted to stay. I lost everything, even custody of my three beautiful sons.

But let me ask another question: Do you believe that any of the following are actually attainable, or do you feel they are beyond your reach?

- Freedom from emotional wounds and wrongs committed against you
- Freedom from worry, frustration, and fear
- Freedom from past mistakes and failures
- Freedom from settling for less or losing yourself
- Freedom from destructive patterns, addictions, and other life-controlling issues
- Freedom from dysfunctional relationships
- Freedom from painful losses
- Freedom from guilt, shame, and regret
- Freedom from… [finish this sentence]

Thankfully, after losing everything I cared about, I moved into the reality of the freedom expressed in this second set of statements!

How do you face the unthinkable? Live through lifelong consequences without losing yourself? Navigate the impossible through faith? Break free from addictions and dysfunctional patterns that keep you bound, stuck, broken, and even hopeless? I did it—one choice at a time. And, over the last twenty years, I have helped many others to do the same.

Let me encourage you that you can do it too. Today, I can personally say, beyond a shadow of a doubt, that freedom *is* possible, and a new beginning awaits *you*.

WHAT FREEDOM IS

Freedom is the place where I now live and the posture I choose to maintain. I used to think freedom was a destination or a goal to achieve. I imagined it was a state of finality that required nothing more from me. But, over the years, I have learned that freedom is a journey we experience throughout our lifetimes.

You've likely heard the expression "Stay in your lane." That saying is often used in a context that seemingly restricts our freedom. But staying in your lane, such as on a highway, can be healthy for yourself and others. It can even save your life. The lane that freedom occupies is not always the fast lane. It's a specific pathway that often requires some tough choices and lots of patience, faith, hope, love, and forgiveness. You can choose to pursue your freedom daily—once choice at a time. When you do this, you will find that you have the courage to attain the healing you need.

BEYOND HELP?

No matter what you are struggling with, take a deep breath right now, my friend. People experience many different feelings and symptoms from the wounds of the past and the pain of the present. Some individuals have told me it feels like they are literally dying from a broken heart. One person shared they felt like they were drowning in a sea of past mistakes. I describe my experience in this way: I was sailing along in the ocean on a calm and beautiful day when, suddenly, a raging tempest unleashed a torrent of waves that pummeled me relentlessly.

I used to say things like, "I have tried everything. I have sought God, and I still can't conquer my addictions, dysfunctional relationships, or deep betrayals. How did I get here? Why do I stay? What is wrong with me? Does God love me? Are my sins and past mistakes unforgivable?"

Perhaps my greatest fear was, "Am I beyond God's reach?" The answer, I found, is "Absolutely not!" God was right there waiting for me. And He is waiting for you too. But it will require you to partner with Him every step of the way. That means letting go and letting God by relinquishing the steering wheel of your life and sliding over into the passenger seat, allowing Him into the driver's position.

UNHEALED WOUNDS

Whether you struggle with life-controlling issues, have committed a wrong that seems unforgivable, or have had wrongs perpetrated against you, if you have wounds that are not healed, they will only fester and worsen. Unhealed hurts produce emotional defeat, dysfunctional ways of loving and living, and addictions of many kinds. They will invade and infect every area of your life.

Throughout my two decades of ministry and leading people into freedom, I have met thousands of women and men who struggled in the ways I have just described. Some were bound by defeat—overcome with shame, guilt, and regret. Others experienced the ever-present pain of having been betrayed. Some had been abused in the vilest of ways. Many were haunted by events that happened more than ten or twenty years ago. A number had prayed for years for a loved one to change their destructive behavior and had lost themselves in the waiting.

Many people feel that once they've made mistakes or bad decisions, or once they've been damaged by others, they can never set their life on a positive course again. If you feel this way, the real answer is that *you can.*

FREEDOM AWAITS YOU

If I told you that, even in the midst of your negative circumstances, freedom awaits you, would you believe me? If you knew there was a way out of the pain of your past, would you get in that lane and follow its path? If you knew that your broken heart could be healed, would you surrender to the challenging process of reaching wholeness?

To enter into a life of freedom, you must allow Jesus, the Great Physician, to make you well and show you how to maintain your health. God deeply desires for you to be healed and whole, but I want to make one thing clear: these days, it seems many people want a quick fix or a bailout for their problems, but that is not reality. A Hollywood movie can get you from crisis to "happily ever after" in a couple of hours. Yet, in real life, there are no shortcuts to wholeness.

I know how hard it is to face the daily challenges of moving forward from a damaging past and the consequences it has brought. For many years, I was naive, thinking that if I just recited my prayer cards, quoted Bible verses, and believed hard enough and long enough, God would evacuate me and my loved ones from our predicament and grant me everything I had prayed for and believingly claimed. But I was immature in my faith and had a lot to learn about persevering and possessing enduring faith. As my faith developed, I discovered that God *is* good all the time; and, *all the time*, God is good—regardless of whether everything around me seems to be falling apart. I've learned how to live my life from a faith perspective even in the absence of earthly proof. Today, I know God is a good Father and my Protector, Provider, and Sustainer, all the time.

DON'T SETTLE FOR LESS!

In the pages of this book, you will find solutions, through real-life application, that will challenge every fiber of your being to not settle for less than God's best for your life. Persevering faith in God will release His power to transform you from being simply a survivor to someone who thrives as an overcomer and victor in Christ. Trusting Him in the hard times can be difficult, but know that He is right there with you, enabling you to move beyond your pain and struggles. Walking with Him daily and embracing His guidance will reveal that when you are weak, He is strong for you. God's Holy Spirit will lift you up in an abiding faith that will grow fuller and stronger each day.

As someone who has experienced—even during times of indescribable heartache—the deep love and great power of God our Father, I write about the hard things and silent sufferings of the people of God, as well as those who don't know Him. I've learned that when secret things are brought to light, darkness flees. God takes our faith, trust, and surrender and then empowers us to persevere and fight our way into the freedom He desires for us. With God, you can conquer your fears, overcome present difficulties, and have victory over the pain of the past.

As you read this book, some of the things I share will challenge you, but know that I love you enough to tell you the truth. You deserve to be released and move forward from whatever or whoever is holding you back. The goal is for you to be set free by experiencing the transforming power of God in practical and powerful ways that change the way you think, how you interpret the world around you, and how you respond. I desire for you to be strong spiritually and emotionally. I want you to know God's peace, which is beyond our human understanding, while fulfilling your destiny and purpose in life. I believe in you and in the power of our living God to revive His promises in your life, for your good and His glory.

God is faithful. His promises are trustworthy. His love is everlasting. He will give you *The Courage to Heal*.

With love, encouragement, and belief in you,
—*Tracy Strawberry*

1

THE CHOICE THAT CHANGED EVERYTHING

Come on, boys, we can't miss this flight!" I shouted to my three sons. We all scrambled out the door, and the boys headed toward my green Ford Explorer. As hurried as we were, when I turned from locking the front door, I froze. I was fixated on their excitement as they climbed into the SUV one by one and got into their seats.

Omar, nine, reached for his seat belt. Eight-year-old twins Austin and Evan fidgeted wildly. All three were laughing and carrying on, thrilled about their upcoming "adventure." I still couldn't move.

"Let's go, Mom!" they wailed with impatience through the SUV's open doors. "Remember, we can't be late!" Forcing a smile, I lumbered toward the vehicle as the weight of the looming consequences of my choices made my legs and feet feel like they were chained and shackled.

After loading the boys' luggage and making sure their seat belts were fastened, I headed to the Fort Lauderdale-Hollywood International Airport. I blasted a collection of their favorite songs, knowing they'd sing along. I wanted to hear their sweet voices one last time.

As off-pitch melodies sailed through the air, tears dripped down my face. Quietly, I relished every note.

My silence did not go unnoticed. One sweet voice punctuated the moment. "Mom, why aren't you singing? You always sing with us!"

Fighting back my tears and hoping my voice wouldn't crack, I said, "I just want to listen to you boys today. You know I love to hear you sing!"

An hour later, the four of us stood at an airline check-in counter.

"And who are these fine young men?" a smiling agent asked.

"These are my three sons, Omar, Austin, and Evan," I said proudly.

"Well, I'm pleased to meet you, boys," the woman replied, still smiling, her attention fixed on my children.

"Nice to meet you!" the three boys chimed in unison, with smiles to match.

"And where are you and your mom going today? Are you going on vacation?" the agent asked.

"No," one of them piped up. Young and innocent, he answered her question with blatant honesty. "We're going to live with my dad. Mom can't come, but she is going to visit us."

My cheeks burned with shame.

With shock written all over her face, the woman turned and looked directly at me. Then, speechless, she immediately withdrew her cheery attention from our family and kept her focus on the computer screen in front of her. Struggling to make eye contact with me, she handed me the boys' tickets and directed us to the gate.

Embarrassed, I forced a smile and waved my children closer. "Come on, boys. Grab your carry-on bags and let's get moving."

I could barely breathe. I couldn't feel my feet as I walked past hundreds of passengers coming and going. I kept telling myself that this was just another visit, and they would be back home soon. The kids chatted away, talking about airplanes and flying and all the fun things they would do with their dad.

"Just another visit, Tracy. Just another visit," I repeated to myself consolingly.

We arrived at the gate at the beginning of the pre-boarding process. A flight attendant hustled toward me. Again, it felt like shackles were tightening around my ankles as I seemingly couldn't put one foot in front of the other. Could I actually put my sons on an airplane with a one-way ticket to live with my ex-husband?

The friendly-faced flight attendant stood before us, smiling. "These must be the three brothers who are flying together today. I'm the airline escort assigned to watch over them." Likely noticing the pained look on my face, she patted me on the arm. "Don't worry, Mom! They'll be in good hands! I will take good care of them."

As I thanked the flight attendant, the boys grabbed my hands and blurted out, "Mommy! Mommy! We gotta pray. We always pray right before we fly!"

As a relatively new Christian, I had recently begun a tradition of holding hands with the boys and praying together with them. My heart aching, I knelt before the three of them. "You're right, we do. Would you like to start?"

The boys took turns, each asking God to bless Mommy and the man flying the airplane. I fought back tears as I listened. It was all I could do to say "Amen." Then, my sons wrapped their tiny arms around me and squeezed as hard as they could. One by one, they kissed my cheek, looked right into my eyes, and, with their big, beautiful smiles, said, "I love you, Mommy!"

The flight attendant who was waiting patiently a few feet away moved closer to us. Almost apologetically, she looked at me and said, "It's time to go."

"Just another visit, Tracy. Just another visit," I half-heartedly told myself.

The boys followed the woman in her pressed uniform. Then, they all turned to look back at me and offer final waves as they moved into the jet bridge, shouting, "See you soon, Mommy! See you soon!"

Smiling, I waved back while holding my breath to stop the flow of tears. "Just another visit, Tracy. Just another visit," I desperately recited under my breath. But really, who was I kidding? I couldn't pretend any longer.

I stared at the backs of my children's heads until I could no longer see them. Yet I couldn't bear to wait for the plane to take off. "I have to get out of here," I said to myself. With tears streaming down my face, I started the long walk out of the terminal toward the parking garage. My superficial veil of denial was melting away as I struggled to remember where I had parked. I began to feel a rush of emotions stemming from a consequence that would play out in my life for years to come.

HAD I FALLEN TOO FAR?

I drove home in a daze. I have no idea how I even got to my house, so overwhelming were my grief and despair. When I pulled into the driveway, I turned the car off. Again, I couldn't move. I stared through the windshield at the front porch where my sons had constantly paraded in and out of our home. I sat in silence. Eerie silence. No singing. No laughter. No high-pitched cries of, "Mommy, he hit me!" or "Mommy, he said something mean!" Nothing but my own ragged breaths.

I dragged myself out of the vehicle, each step heavier than the last. As I opened the front door to the house, my gaze dropped to the floor. My stomach churned when I caught sight of little-boy sneakers and flip-flops that I had forgotten to pack. The sight of those tiny shoes shattered any last remnants of my denial.

It wasn't just another visit. They weren't *ever* coming back.

My world obliterated, I collapsed onto the floor. Curled up in a fetal position, clutching the little shoes to my chest, I sobbed uncontrollably. I just lay there, mired in self-loathing and self-pity, my tears dripping onto the cool tile. I felt worthless and hopeless. A while later, the tears ran dry. Utterly spent, I fell asleep on the floor.

Hours later, I opened my eyes. The front door was wide open, and my keys were still in the lock. My fingers still curled around the shoes, I forced myself up. The quietness thundered as I made my way to my bedroom and crawled into bed. Exhausted but wide awake, I stared at the ceiling, listening to the rhythmic whoosh of the fan swirling above. At some point, I dozed off again, seemingly smothered by my heavy heart.

When I awoke, it was dark. My heart thumped wildly. Anxiety exploded when I realized the same agonizing reality had not changed: my sons were gone.

Unable to endure the dreadful silence, I walked over to my neighbor's house where my dear friend Laura and her husband, Steve, lived. They were like my "home away from home" parents. When Laura answered the door, I didn't have to say a word. She pulled me to her and held me close while I sobbed onto her shoulder. "It's going to be okay, honey," Laura assured me. "You are going to get through this, I promise. Steve and I are here for you." I spent the night at their house. I couldn't bear to be alone.

What made my loss even more painful was that this happened after I had repented of my sins and committed my life to following Jesus Christ. My boys had placed their trust in Jesus too. I had been clean from drugs and sober from alcohol for almost two years and was growing in my relationship with the Lord. Previously, my life had been in ruins. I had been divorced twice and had three children I deeply loved but could barely care for emotionally.

I had fervently prayed that God would grant me custody of the boys by court order so we could continue to grow together in our newfound relationship with Jesus. We had been baptized together and were attending church weekly and memorizing Bible verses. Surely, God would want my sons to live with me so they could grow up in His ways and be able to learn His Word. After all, they happened to be about the same age I had been when pure evil lived next door to where I grew up, devastating my life for years to come. (In later chapters, I will explain more about this situation, how it affected me, and how God healed me.) Wouldn't it help for my sons to learn to trust in God when faced with difficulties and dangers? And didn't I finally deserve a break?

But my attorney advised me that the judge overseeing the custody hearing would rule that my bad choices to date far outweighed my present good choices, leaving my reputation extremely compromised in the court's opinion. I didn't want to put my sons through a bitter trial in which they would relive my past mistakes—a trial that my attorney and the courts fully convinced me I would lose. Foster care would be the route for them if I fought for custody, and, in the end, custody would be granted to their father anyway. To prevent my sons from experiencing a horrifying ordeal of being put in foster care and completely displaced, I relented and signed over my rights to custody.

Living in a different state from my parents and other family members, unemployable, and battling to believe that a new life could be possible for someone like me, I felt defeated. At thirty years of age, I thought I was too old to make up for all my mistakes. I had fallen too far. I had destroyed too much. My heart felt like it was broken beyond repair.

But it wasn't. I would soon find out that I had the courage to heal—a courage that comes from God alone. And I want you to know that you can find the courage to heal as well.

DISCOVERING THE ROOT ISSUE

The Courage to Heal is not focused on overcoming alcohol addiction and drug abuse alone. It conveys portions of my story that detail my former struggles, yet it will engage you within the midst of your own particular difficulties. This book is about overcoming your harmful habits, your past, and your pain—no matter what struggles are involved. Everyone has been offended, rejected, and hurt emotionally or physically in some way. No one is exempt from the pain, disappointment, or heartache that comes from a betrayal, a breakup, a loss, a disappointment, a failure, or a surrender to temptation to do something wrong.

Before I became sober, I had tried several times to quit drinking and using drugs on my own, to no avail. I just could not stop! But when I finally made the choice to change, applying the principles I will unfold in this book, I was enabled to turn my life around. Even so, after twenty-one years of sobriety and the wonderful freedom I have experienced, I still consider myself in recovery because, like anyone else, I have to daily continue to make right choices for myself. And I am fully committed to doing that.

This book gets down to the "root causes" of why people get entangled in addictions of every sort and enslaved in life patterns that cause dysfunctional living and loving. If you have ever participated in counseling or therapy of any kind, you've probably been told by your counselor or therapist that "the problem isn't the problem." The issues that lead someone to seek counseling are usually symptoms or manifestations of a much deeper problem. For me, my addiction to drugs and alcohol was the result of my trying to cope with emotional and physical pain, frustration, fear, and disillusionment.

For you, the symptom may be overeating that is threatening your health. It might be gambling or a lack of financial discipline that is resulting in serious problems in your daily living or within your marriage. Perhaps it is heartache from a betrayal or a negative past event you can't leave behind. It might be a debilitating emotion such as fear or anxiety that holds you back from your breakthrough and keeps you from experiencing God's very best for your life. It may be a relationship that no longer seems to have life within it. You might be praying or waiting for a loved one to break free from addiction or another dysfunctional pattern, or to love you back—to the point that you may feel like you're losing yourself waiting for them to find themselves.

These scenarios are all evidence of internal problems, my friend. We must get down to the primary issues. Again, debilitating behaviors or emotions are an outward expression of internal dysfunction. It is how your brokenness, pain, or inner struggles reveal themselves.

> **DEBILITATING BEHAVIORS OR EMOTIONS ARE AN OUTWARD EXPRESSION OF INTERNAL DYSFUNCTION.**

COURAGE AND HEALING

I couldn't possibly know the heart of every person who will read these words, but God does. He knows every detail of your life, and I don't think it is a coincidence or an accident that you're reading this book. God desires for you to move beyond whatever is holding you back from your greatness or hindering your potential from being realized. He has goals for you to achieve and dreams for you to fulfill. He has good purposes and plans for you to live out. You may have lost your desire to dream, or you may have a goal in your heart right now that has been dormant for years, just waiting for you to find the courage to heal and move forward.

The word *courage* means "the quality of mind or spirit that enables a person to face difficulty, danger, pain, etc., without fear; bravery." An old-fashioned meaning of the word, which I still find significant to this topic, is "the heart as the source of emotion."[1] What powerful definitions! To have courage means to become able in the face of adversity. Courage also refers to the heart, which we will address quite a bit throughout this book. Do you see the power-enabling words in these meanings—"the quality of your mind or spirit" and "the heart as your source of emotion"—that enables you to face your difficulty, hardship, or pain?

According to these definitions, when we get our heart, mind, and spirit right, we will heal! Among the meanings of the verb *heal* are "to make healthy, whole, or sound; restore to health; free from ailment"; "mend; get well."[2]

Having the courage to heal necessitates bravery. You will be required to make choices and take steps even though you are afraid, apathetic, or unmotivated. Bravery is not the absence of fear but the ability to move forward in the midst of fear. You will have to advance with great force and movement until you have broken through the barricade to freedom. That's called *breakthrough*, and you're worth it!

CHANGE IS POSSIBLE!

You may have reached a point in your life where you feel that change is impossible for you. I have been there. Here are some choices that helped me to break the cyclical pattern keeping me bound.

STOP THE BLAME GAME AND DIG DEEP WITHIN YOURSELF

Truth be told, for years, I lived within a severe state of denial, refusing to believe or admit I had a problem with drugs and alcohol. There are no words to describe my stubbornness, selfishness, and self-pity. I wallowed in

---

1. *Dictionary.com*, s.v. "courage," https://www.dictionary.com/browse/courage.
2. *Dictionary.com*, s.v. "heal," https://www.dictionary.com/browse/heal.

my mess for years, blaming everyone and anything else, refusing to look at myself and dig deep to find the answers that would set me free.

Did you catch that? Stopping the blame game and digging deep within yourself is key. Own your stuff and deal with it, friend. No one else owns your destiny but you and God. Refuse to give it away or settle for less than what God desires for you.

Countless opportunities for help and change were offered to me, but, until I made the choice to accept the help I needed, I pushed all those opportunities away, saying (or thinking), "I've got this! I don't need anyone's help! I'm not like so-and-so! I can quit anytime! I'll do it my way." Sound familiar? One of the many lessons I've learned on my journey to healing and wholeness is that you cannot trudge the road to freedom alone, regardless of who you think you are or what's holding you back. God created us for relationship, fellowship, and support for a reason. Help must accompany hope. Practical application, encouragement, and accountability are keys to attaining any victory!

LEARN TO RECOGNIZE TRUTH FROM LIES

What often makes our situation even more challenging is that we have a spiritual adversary named Satan who opposes human beings because he is God's enemy, and he fights against the image of God in us. (See Genesis 1:26–27; 1 Peter 5:8.) Our enemy tries to plant lies in our minds in an attempt to influence us through a spirit of defeat. When we unknowingly listen to these lies, it can lead us to self-justification in which we dress up denial to look like truth.

Denial and codependency were my blinders. These blinders were so thick I couldn't distinguish lies from truth, counterfeit from real. Meanwhile, the damage I was doing to myself, my children, my extended family, and others was obvious to everyone but me. I had deluded myself with "stinking thinking" evidenced by my self-destructive choices. My erratic behavior and constant manipulation to justify those behaviors created an endless cycle of pain, fear, and worry for myself and my loved ones.

My greatest fear was of losing custody of my children—or dying. What if my sons' last memory of me alive left them with an unfulfilled longing for a loving relationship with me? In either scenario, they would be left without their mother. But I fell so far down the scale that I no longer cared what happened to me. That is a telltale sign you are deep in your addiction or despair, whatever it may be. The desire to isolate turns into the norm, and, before you know it, you are shut in and shutting everyone else out. You are existing behind locked doors and runaway spaces where no one can find you to nag or judge you.

The darkness became something I longed for because I couldn't face the light. The lie became my reality because the truth seemed too hard to bear. Honesty became untouchable, a dream that could never be my reality. Truth was a word that accompanied great pain because if I dared to face it, I would see the reality of who I was and what I was doing to myself and those around me. I couldn't handle that thought. In reality, the truth is ever present, whether you choose to embrace it or not. It's not going away. Denial is death, but acknowledging the truth is life. I tricked myself into believing denial was easier than facing the pain of honesty that would set me free. Denial is a false sense of safety that has no standard to live up to or accountability from others to face. Again, it keeps you hiding from a truth that never goes away.

CHOOSE HOPE AND HELP

Even after two years of sobriety, I had to face one of my worst fears: losing custody of my sons. It could have been different, but it wasn't. I could have listened, but I didn't. I could have and should have received help years earlier, but I didn't. I realized that I couldn't alter the past, but I could change my present, my future, and the future of my children by choosing hope and help. I could make the decision to live a new life by getting out of my own way and coming to the end of myself. Thankfully, two years before the heartbreaking day when I faced the unthinkable head-on and surrendered custody of my children, I had yielded to that hope and help and had begun the healing process. It was one of the best choices I have ever made, and it set me up for greater ones to follow.

Allow me to take you back a bit to the moment when my blinders of denial were stripped from my eyes, paving the way for my recovery to begin. I was on the phone with my dear friend Lisa, who had already been in recovery for several years. Lisa was listening to me ever so intently as I shared with her my overwhelming fear that I was going to lose custody of my children. I could not shake this reality from my heart or mind. It was embedded in the very depths of my soul. It was an ever-present fear that consumed me.

At the time, I didn't realize that God was giving me a clear warning before the actual event took place. I didn't know He was cautioning me to turn away from the destructive life I was living without Him and to turn to Him for the new life He had waiting for me all along. I was in the middle of my second divorce and overwhelmed by fear. The collapse of my life was in full swing.

Lisa continued to listen patiently as I shared my worry and despair. After I ran out of words, she calmly asked me if I was ready to hear some deep truth. Trusting her and the love she had for me, I said yes. With a calm yet bold delivery, she told me I was just like her. Then she paused. The silence was deafening and caught my attention. I asked her what she meant by that statement, and she went on to say, "Tracy, you are an alcoholic and a drug addict. You are just like me. The details of our stories are different, but the outcome is the same. The only difference is that I have surrendered to the truth and made the choice to change. I'm offering you the opportunity to do the same. Will you take it?"

I sat there dumbfounded, with another God-opportunity placed before me to receive the help I desperately needed. I asked Lisa, "What do I have to do?" She told me about a meeting that would start at seven that evening in a park that was close to my house. I didn't need a babysitter because the boys had just left to spend the summer with their dad in Puerto Rico. It was part of our divorce decree at the time. I had no reason or excuse not to attend. Lisa went on to tell me that she couldn't be there, but she had the name of a woman she wanted me to call as soon as we got off the phone. This woman's name was Laura. Yes, you guessed it. It was the same Laura who opened her front door to me the very night I had to surrender custody of my sons.

Immediately after my phone call with Lisa, I stared at Laura's phone number. I had written it down on one of my bills, all of which were stacked on the counter. Help was right before me, and, this time, I made the choice to step into it. I made the phone call to Laura. She answered and, with a sweet, welcoming voice, said to me, "I've been waiting for you to call, honey, and I'm so glad you did."

Waiting for me to call? I found out that Lisa had already talked to Laura about me months earlier. You see, friend, God is always working on our behalf. My denial did not stop Him from setting up a solution for me. He placed me on the hearts of people whom He would use to help and support me through this life-changing journey on which I was about to embark.

Laura told me she would be waiting for me at the meeting. And she was right there to greet me as soon as I walked up. There I was, amid a circle of people who were laughing, hugging, and sharing about their days as they waited for the meeting to commence. Order was called, the rules were read, and then, one by one, people started voluntarily sharing about their lives. That evening, I heard story after story of the destruction, pain, and problems—and also the profound victories and hope—in their journeys. There was not one element of someone's struggle that I could not relate to. I felt deep empathy and compassion for every person who shared about their life.

Could it be that I was "one of them" (as if they were a different breed of people)? My ignorance was not bliss, and, I have to admit, it was downright shameful. Before this point, I hadn't known the true meaning of alcoholism or addiction. I had thought addiction affected only a certain demographic or type of person. That demographic or type certainly wasn't me. Like many people, I'd held a horrific stereotype that "these kinds of people" were just losers. They were individuals who made excuses for their lives and chose that path. They were criminals and homeless people, not regular people like me. People like that came from dysfunctional homes, and I had not. I'd had a stable upbringing.

God forgive me for my ignorance. I was trying to justify myself right out of the reality that I was just like they were—someone who was suffering, not an outcast misplaced in this world. In my more than twenty years of sobriety, I have come to learn that almost everyone who takes the first step to surrender by admitting they are afflicted with the stronghold of addiction has about the same stereotypical attitude or ignorance I had. I had tried to compare my story to others as a way to justify myself right out of the label of defeat. I didn't want to be an addict or an alcoholic. What a label! What an identity! I didn't want it. Who would?

Let me be clear: addiction, or any other diagnosis or struggle you may be dealing with, is not who you are. It's not your identity. Instead, it is a stronghold that you are choosing to overcome. It's not a label you paste on yourself in hopes it will keep you on the straight and narrow through fear and shame. Addiction of any kind is an inward brokenness expressing itself through the outward behavior of drug abuse, alcoholism, or another life-controlling issue, behavior, or emotion. As I emphasized earlier, the issue is the symptom, not the real problem.

> **ADDICTION, OR ANY OTHER DIAGNOSIS OR STRUGGLE YOU MAY BE DEALING WITH, IS NOT WHO YOU ARE. IT'S NOT YOUR IDENTITY. INSTEAD, IT IS A STRONGHOLD THAT YOU ARE CHOOSING TO OVERCOME.**

ACCEPT WHO YOU WERE CREATED TO BE

The battle over any debilitating habit can be won. You don't have to wear a label of defeat, and I beg you not to do so. As I mentioned earlier, even though I consider myself still in recovery, the greeting "Hello, my name is Tracy, and I'm an addict" will never cross my lips again. If someone is diagnosed with the disease of cancer, you do not hear them say, "Hi, my name is Tracy, and I am cancer." It is a concept that is taught in hopes of removing denial from the affliction of addiction that people suffer. I understand where the concept came from, but I believe it is a deception and a label of defeat that no one should wear.

Life-controlling issues did not dictate God's creation of you and who He designed you to be. He did not create you in defeat! You were "*fearfully and wonderfully made*" by Him. (See Psalm 139:14, various translations.) You were made by God in His image. That's a powerful statement, one that holds the weight of the truth it professes!

God spoke: "Let us make human beings in our image, make them reflecting our nature so they can be responsible for the fish in the sea, the birds in the air, the cattle, and, yes, Earth itself, and every animal that moves on the face of Earth." God created human beings; he created them godlike, reflecting God's nature. He created them male and female. God blessed them: "Prosper! Reproduce! Fill Earth! Take charge! Be responsible for fish in the sea and birds in the air, for every living thing that moves on the face of Earth." (Genesis 1:26–28 MSG)

God not only created us in His image, but He also created us for His mighty purposes. God did not create us with destruction or dysfunctional loving and living in mind. Quite the contrary. He created us for relationship with Him and to be His ambassadors of reconciliation. When God commissioned Adam and Eve to be responsible for the fish in the sea and all the creatures of the earth, He set human beings apart as the pinnacle of His creation. He made us powerful in Him to rule and reign over this earth and everything in it. Simply put, sin, shame, pain, regret, fear, anxiety, dysfunction, or defeat of any kind doesn't have to get the final say in our lives.

God created us with a void that only He can fill. And when we allow God to fill that void, He empowers us through His Spirit to overcome our sinful nature. We are powerful when our lives are submitted to God. He wants you and me to be blessed and to prosper, reproduce, fill the earth, and lead others to Him. His divine blueprint for our lives is beyond anything we can fathom, dream, or imagine. My destiny, along with that of countless others, had been derailed by the enemy of darkness. I had allowed that enemy, Satan, to be in control of my life for far too long. It was time to take back my power and my life. It's your time too.

I have learned the truth that I am an overcomer in Christ Jesus. Addiction is a battle I have won through the power of God and the process of change. Still, I need to safeguard my heart for the rest of my life to ensure I do not relapse into that life of darkness and defeat. Once you give your life to Christ, you are forgiven; you are a child of God who has been given a clean slate and a fresh start to begin again. I was clean and sober for one year before giving my life to Christ. My newfound relationship with the Lord enabled me not only to *stay* clean and sober but also to discover and fulfill the good plans God has for my life. That certainly didn't happen overnight, as I'll explain in more detail in coming chapters.

The Bible says in Proverbs 18:21 that life and death are in the power of the tongue. Again, when you define yourself as an addict, an alcoholic, or a dysfunctional individual in any other way—or allow anyone other than God to define you—you are embracing and claiming defeat as your identity. Your addiction or dysfunction is not who you are. It is not your destiny or a lifelong sentence you have been condemned to serve. It is a battle that you can win if you put the work in to achieve your victory.

You win this battle when you choose to let go of self-reliance and self-will, place your trust in Jesus and dedicate your life to Him, and let Him work within you and on your behalf. As I mentioned previously, it took me a while to get to a place of spiritual surrender to God through faith in His Son, Jesus Christ. I knew I needed to move forward in solution, so I chose to take a physical step first. As I described, my healing journey started with a phone call of surrender to an amazing woman named Laura. She gave me direction, and I followed it.

THE CHOICES WE MAKE

The focus of this book is largely centered on the profound reality that—for better or worse, in times of resting faith or persevering faith—the daily choices we make determine the trajectory of our lives and our healing journey. Our choices can set us up for success or failure, healing or heartache, peace or torment, life or death. These choices can position us to experience God's favor and blessing or enslave us to a cycle of sin and dysfunction. And since no one lives in a vacuum, the choices we make often have a ripple effect on our family members, friends, neighbors, coworkers, bystanders, and passersby. The decisions people make can shape genealogies and civilizations for generations, leaving a legacy that endures. We are not immune to the consequences of our choices or those of others. Yet you have the power to leave a brand-new legacy for yourself and your loved ones through a faith that dominates and perseveres through all things. We serve a God of yet another chance, a fresh start, a new beginning, a new life!

Remember, I made two major decisions that changed everything in my life. The first was to deny I needed help and try to do things my way. This was an ongoing decision, and I paid a high price for my stubbornness and rebellion. I ruined my life for years and destroyed nearly everything that was important to me. The second choice was to admit I needed help and actively seek out that help. That choice was really in two stages—first admitting my addictions and then admitting my need for Jesus Christ. And it involved the process I just described: (1) stop the blame game and dig deep within yourself for the origin of your struggles; (2) learn to recognize truth from lies, counterfeit from real; (3) choose hope and help; and (4) accept who you were created to be in God through Christ.

This choice still awaits you amid your struggle or pain: the choice to come to the end of yourself, surrender the way you have been doing things, and embrace the healing journey, which is the pathway to freedom. You see, my deepest shame, pain, guilt, and regret are *not* the end of my story. The beauty about an ending is that it leads you right into a new beginning.

This is not the last chapter of the book, nor the last chapter of your life. You can choose to begin again, my friend. It's not over. We've only just begun. I know you have the courage to heal. Let's keep going!

COURAGE CHOICES FOR YOUR HEALING

1. Has the "blame game" hindered you from taking a close look at yourself in order to heal? If so, whom or what do you blame? Why are you giving that person or thing so much power over your life? Begin to take your power and life back by making the choice to dig deep within yourself and acknowledge the source(s) of what is holding you back from healing. Get to the root, friend! Own your own "stuff" so you can be set free.

2. Is it difficult for you to distinguish truth from lies? What lies might you currently be believing—or have you believed in the past—that are causing you harm? List the "fake/counterfeit" people or things you have elevated to "real" status in your life. How has this affected you and your destiny? Now, search this chapter and pull out some powerful truths and realities you can believe, embrace, and live out.

3. Write down some ways in which you can choose hope and help for your life.

4. According to the biblical principles in this chapter, who does God say that you are? List the Scripture references included and write down truths from these passages that will begin to set you free. You are worth it!

2

WHEN THE TEMPTATION TO QUIT COMES CALLING

I found comfort in the recovery community as I received the support of my new friends there. As I described in chapter 1, I took a physical step of surrender when I called Laura and attended my first recovery meeting. Months later, I would finally acknowledge that I needed to take a far greater step, a spiritual one that would require a leap of faith. But it would be a while before I was ready for that spiritual adventure. For the time being, I attended recovery meetings with Laura as my sponsor. I received counseling once a week and went to meetings every day. I had my routine and was faithfully working my program.

Fast-forward twelve months. I was about to celebrate being clean and sober from drugs and alcohol for a full year. That sounds great, doesn't it? But I was also now ready to completely call it quits on my recovery. You might wonder why I would want to quit after achieving this success and beginning to turn my life around. It was because a goal of chasing sobriety wasn't enough for me if it didn't also heal the underlying issues that had driven me to abuse alcohol and drugs in the first place. It was as if I had to continually white-knuckle my way through life. My recovery program, however initially helpful, wasn't solving the deep hurts and inner despair that continually plagued me. It couldn't make me right with God, heal me, or make me whole.

Sometimes I went to meetings two or three times a day, working the steps of secular recovery with a sponsor, yet I was still enslaved to my addiction's curse. My cravings for the next high or euphoric escape were constantly trolling and stalking me everywhere I went. I had adopted the concept of acknowledging a "Higher Power," but I still refused to hear anything about Jesus and the Holy Spirit or to serve the one true living God through a saving faith in Jesus Christ. I would not take the spiritual step I so desperately needed to become healed and whole. I continued to pray to God, whom I had rejected. In reality, I had created my own god, and then wondered why I couldn't receive answers or obtain results. It was as if nothing or no one was hearing or answering me, or else they just didn't care to heal me.

Those were my gut-level, honest feelings. I felt like I was worse off than on the day of my first surrender to swear off addictive substances and change my ways. The battle was fierce. The desire to relapse was breathing down my neck and whispering in my ear twenty-four hours a day, seven days a week. The pain of my past constantly haunted my present, and I could not break free from the torture. All I wanted was a peaceful escape.

To truly break free, I needed the Spirit of God and His power through Jesus Christ. I was trying to heal without the Healer. If I could go back and change one major thing in my life, it would be to surrender to Jesus when I was first told about Him. When I was young, I went to the altar at a salvation service to receive Christ, but it didn't stay with me. I also responded to altar calls on several other occasions over the years, but I didn't understand I needed to make a commitment to Jesus. I also needed to be discipled, to learn about Christ and grow in Him. Everyone has their own journey, but I lost so much by denying Him as long as I did. I wasn't living for Christ and accessing His healing power. Because of this, the absence of my addiction-enabled euphoria only magnified the emptiness in my life. Yet, as I began to describe in the previous chapter, Jesus was always waiting for me and placing people and solutions in my life in spite of my rejection of Him. He just kept loving and pursuing me.

I had made up my mind that on the day of my one-year anniversary of sobriety, I was going to say thank you, pick up my commemorative chip and key chain—and then disappear. Chips and key chains are tokens awarded in recovery to celebrate increments of time you have achieved in sobriety. But I was ready to trash those achievements and retreat to my old life of denial, darkness, and destruction.

My one-year sobriety anniversary was supposed to be a huge milestone of achievement. My parents were flying from St. Louis, Missouri, to Boca Raton, Florida, to celebrate me and this grand accomplishment that none of us had believed would ever happen. My sponsor was so proud of me. My recovery friends were excited for me. And the young ladies I was sponsoring in the program were inspired by my dedication, discipline, and perseverance. But all of that still wasn't enough to fill the void in my heart. The pain was too great, and the hopelessness was on overdrive. If I was going to continue to feel this way, without any lasting peace, then what was the point of doing what was right? The payoff of being sober and drug-free just didn't seem worth the incessant torture caused by my quest for freedom.

In my mind, there was no relief in sight. No release. No break. The consequences of my addiction were overwhelming. I was losing the battle for custody of my three sons, and my financial debt was too deep for me to even dare to believe for a breakthrough. Guilt, shame, and regret consumed me. My work opportunities included waiting tables and telemarketing, jobs in which I would never be able to earn enough to pay the bills. All seemed lost, with no way out. My pile of "stuff" was too deep and too heavy to carry. I felt as if I couldn't buy a win even if I had all the money in the world.

I couldn't pretend any longer. I wasn't going to make it. My mind was made up: "I'm out. Done!"

Have you ever been in a dark place where you felt like quitting? Just giving up? Caving, bailing, and reversing course to seek after a seemingly easier, softer, less challenging way of doing things? Have you arrived at the point in your journey where victory and breakthrough no longer seem worth the discipline and fight required to win the battle?

These feelings are normal to experience but dangerous to give in to. Don't be fooled by an illusion that you can have a "magic carpet ride" enabling you to glide over your problems—such a magic carpet is actually a body bag. Whether you're dealing with a habit you can't seem to break, an addiction you need to overcome, someone or something you should let go of, a relationship trial, or an emotional or mental struggle, don't surrender to the pain. Don't quit. Stay your course, my friend! You're worth the victory that awaits you.

REACH OUT FOR SUPPORT IN DARK TIMES

Somehow, even during my darkest hours, I kept putting into practice steps I had learned in recovery, such as calling a person in your support group when you feel you want to quit or check out of the process. So, I did just that. *Please do not miss what I just said.* If you continue to do what is right and put into practice all the "lifeline" tools, you *will* make it.

Witnessing the joy and unwavering support of my parents at my sobriety celebration provided me with the glimmer of hope I needed to take my focus off my pain and regret. Prior to that day, I had been estranged from my parents for about eight years. Over those years, they had tried to stay connected with me, but I didn't reciprocate. Yet here they were, beaming with pride over my sobriety and thankful to God for the opportunity to finally be a part of my life again. When my mother asked for the microphone to say a few words, it was as if God was speaking through her. "This is our daughter," she said. "She's not an addict to us. She's our daughter."

Hearing that powerful declaration, I felt human, normal, accepted, favored, and loved for the first time in what seemed like forever. And, in that moment, I started to understand how my parents' unconditional love and unwavering support was a picture of how God had been pursuing me relentlessly throughout my period of rebellion. God loved me. God was fighting for me. God was trying to rescue me, heal me, and make me whole. Little did my parents know how dangerously close I had come to running away from them and God once again. But God knew the depth of my pain, and He was throwing me another lifeline through the encouragement and support of my godly parents.

Let me encourage you with this thought: whatever it may be that derails you—whether substance abuse or something else—you can starve that debilitating practice. The all-consuming desire to feed your addiction, bad habit, or hindering life pattern will eventually pass if you continue to starve what defeats you. Starve your fear and frustration. I'm so glad I didn't check out that day and call it quits. If I had, I would have destroyed one of the greatest celebrations I have ever experienced, not only for myself but for my loved ones as well.

Don't listen to the lies of the enemy telling you that you're unworthy and beyond saving. Reject that quitting spirit. Don't accept defeat but keep forging ahead. Reach out to your support system during dark times. (If you don't have a support system of people to turn to, start building one today.) The false accusations and self-loathing don't have to win the day.

> **DON'T LISTEN TO THE LIES OF THE ENEMY TELLING YOU THAT YOU'RE UNWORTHY AND BEYOND SAVING. DON'T ACCEPT DEFEAT BUT KEEP FORGING AHEAD.**

LOOK FOR THE PEOPLE GOD SENDS YOUR WAY

My experience of almost throwing away all the progress I had made illustrated for me that, while the practical tools I had been using to stay sober were beneficial, I needed something more to change my appetite and life patterns. I just didn't know exactly what I was missing. At that time, I was still trying to heal through human efforts instead of the healing power of Jesus Christ.

About a week after my sobriety celebration, I called a close friend from support group. My struggle and emotional torment had returned as the feelings of joy from my celebration wore off. This friend of mine, whom I'll call Sara, had pulled herself away from the throes of addiction. She responded to my desperation by reminding me of how destructive it is to retreat to that familiar place of darkness. Then she gave me a very specific task to follow. She told me to go to the 1:00 p.m. recovery meeting at a location she and I often frequented together during the day. I was to keep an eye out for a mature woman with salt-and-pepper hair whose name was Kim. "How is she going to know who I am?" I asked Sara. She responded, "Oh, she will know."

I attended that meeting, but when it ended, I didn't see a woman with salt-and-pepper hair anywhere. I anxiously started toward the door, and then I saw her, leaning against the old panel walls of the hallway. She confidently positioned herself in front of me, looked me straight in the eyes, and spoke—with authority, yet with a thread of love—"You must be Tracy."

"Yes," I responded. "How did you know?"

She said, "I know that look of despair and desperation well."

Kim was obviously a no-nonsense woman, a straight shooter. No sugarcoating in her veins. She spoke firmly, and her words cut deep, yet God knew what and who I needed. I was tough and almost impossible to deal with most of the time. Strong-willed and unbridled, my emotions led the way. Most of the time, a fiery feeling would rise up inside me, and I would let it be known. I was a force to be reckoned with, and God knew my game. So, He sent me a force more powerful than myself.

I can't overemphasize the point that God is continually working on our behalf. He will always send the help and support we need, regardless of the situation. Have you had people in your life repeatedly bring up a pattern, characteristic, reaction, or condition within you that is hurting you or stopping your progress in life? It may be relationship patterns you remain bound to, debilitating emotions that consume you, or other life situations that control you. Regardless of what it is, God will always send the people you need and the solution required to help you break free.

Will you recognize the help when it shows up? Will you choose to accept it when offered? I highly recommend not waiting as long as I did to say yes to the help God sends your way. Remember, I had every excuse for refusing to accept various offers of help. I blamed everyone except myself. I refused to take direction, opting to continue in my own ways. It was up to me to receive the assistance, then take the necessary action steps to experience the change I needed.

Once I knew the action steps, I had to exercise the courage to follow through with them. Knowing and doing are two separate concepts. Dreams become realities through the "doing." You will experience freedom when you move forward and take action. Only then can the healing begin. Have you written down any necessary steps you already know to follow in order to see change take place in yourself and your situation? How will you move forward in them? What would be your very first step toward the breakthrough you need? The steps will be challenging but necessary.

Another roadblock to my healing was my lack of perseverance. If a miracle of help didn't come immediately or things didn't change quickly, I wanted to quit. I was at that very crossroads on the day I met Kim. She asked me where I was going when I left the meeting. When I told her I didn't know, she challenged me, saying, "Yes, you do, Tracy. What are you thinking? You're thinking about calling it quits, throwing in the towel? Entering into another dreadful relationship that will lead to more destructive life consequences for you?" She continued, "Tracy, I understand. I've been there." In one long sentence, she talked about how she had slept around, shot heroin, smoked crack—and then discovered the love of Jesus. I was stunned. But her words were just what I needed to hear.

What's your situation, friend? What's holding you back? What's tempting you to remain stuck or to quit on yourself and your life? Perhaps you can't relate to being a slave to raging addictions. But let me ask you: where does God need to release the pressure that is smothering you? Do you long to take a deep breath followed by a soul-cleansing exhalation that discharges the stress and anxiety emanating from your core? How long have you been stuck, broken, or frustrated? Bound to life-controlling issues or self-destructive patterns? Held captive to a loved one who doesn't want to be well or change their ways? Acknowledge your situation, whatever it may be. Keep reading to learn how to breathe the breath of life. You may feel that deep breaths are in short supply right now, but there is a way to exhale your doubt, fear, lack of confidence, and damaged self-esteem. In the following chapters, you'll learn how to breathe in your value and get your second wind.

THE "JESUS THING"

Kim had my attention. However, I was a little shaken by her mention of the "Jesus thing" because I was angry at God. I didn't want to hear what Kim was saying; nonetheless, I was drawn to her. Later, I would come to understand that it was the Holy Spirit inside her, with the great love of God, drawing me to Him. God was using Kim in a mighty way to help rescue my soul, just as He had used my parents to help save me from nearly self-destructing on the day of my sobriety celebration.

Kim was a mighty woman of God, filled with the Holy Spirit and a boldness for Jesus Christ. Her mission was to go into the rooms of recovery and lead women to Christ. She knew our pain, shame, and resistance to God. She never mentioned church because women and men "like us" would run for the hills before darkening the door of a house of worship. She wasn't a Bible-thumper, but she led me into God's Word before I even knew what was happening. She had great wisdom and discernment in how to help hurting people.

I thank God for men and women who obey the Lord and continue to witness, even to the roughest and toughest of women such as I was. Back then, I would have cursed you out at the sound of Jesus's name. Crazy, right? Today, I love Jesus with all my heart. But, during that time, my struggles, hurts from being betrayed, and turbulent emotions over the consequences occurring in my life were very raw and real. I blamed God for everything that was wrong in my life. I blamed Him for not rescuing me out of sexual abuse when I was a child. I blamed Him for the many other negative things that had happened in my life as I continued to spiral out of control. I blamed Him for not delivering me instantly from my addictions and destructive lifestyles. I blamed Him for the evil that others had perpetrated against me. I blamed Him for my choices to reject the truth and my refusal to take ownership of my actions. The words *admit, submit,* and *change* were not yet part of my vocabulary.

I am so thankful that God never stops pursuing us with His great love. He is constantly calling us to Himself so He can lead us on the pathway to freedom and make us whole, regardless of our situation or issue. He sent Laura to me to begin this process through the recovery program, but I was still rejecting His other messengers and solutions for help. I cried out to

Him in my need, but I kept refusing to grab on to His lifeline or embrace His answers.

Finally, as I stood before Kim, I made the decision that I would choose to "let go and let God." No more arguing or leveraging excuses. I listened to and followed her directions. I was tired of being bitter and broken. This is another key to breakthrough: recognize that it is an ongoing process. Every day, we need to make *right* choices and decisions that take us in the *right* direction for our lives. *Right* equals *right*! It results in power, healing, and freedom.

Kim told me to meet her at a specific café at 5:30 p.m. sharp. She didn't ask if I could make it, was busy, had a babysitter, or any other question. At 5:30, I walked through the door of the café. Kim was sitting there, waiting for me with two cups of coffee and a smile on her face. I was ready to crawl out of my skin. I was so full of anxiety that I wanted to throw up. And yet, for the first time, I didn't want to run away. I wanted to proceed in the right direction. I wanted to be well physically, emotionally, and spiritually.

LISTENING TO THE RIGHT VOICE

For about an hour, Kim and I had a very powerful conversation about how I could move forward with my life. Then she looked down at her watch and abruptly said, "Grab your coffee"—it was my fourth cup—"and let's go." I asked her where we were going, and when she said, "A prayer meeting," I stopped dead in my tracks. "Here we go with the Jesus thing," I thought. I knew it. As she held the door, she looked back at me and said, "Tracy, *step forward*. You still have more to lose, even though you feel as if you've lost it all. Trust me."

Yikes! What a powerful yet triggering word: *trust*. Deep down, I knew she was right. I didn't give myself any time to talk myself out of going to the prayer meeting. I made the choice to take that *step forward* and to *trust* her. We climbed into our separate vehicles, and off we went.

I had about fifteen minutes alone in my SUV to change my mind, turn around, and refuse God's saving help and power once again. I didn't know it at the time, but there was a spiritual battle going on within me. Through the Holy Spirit, God was leading me into a breakthrough, a brand-new life.

But Satan, the prince of the air (see Ephesians 2:2 KJV), who is a liar, thief, and murderer (see John 8:44; 10:10), was trying to hold me captive in my despair and darkness. It was as if the angel of the Lord was on one shoulder, and the devil was on the other. Finally, I listened to the right voice and made the correct choice. I decided to let "right" have its way even though everything in me felt so wrong. I didn't bow down to my emotions, such as fear or anxiety. Without realizing or understanding it, I was listening to God and allowing faith to lead me, even though I was still spiritually blind.

When we arrived at the prayer meeting, I felt a spark of victory within me just for being there. It had taken great courage for me to show up at the café. It had taken great courage for me to follow Kim to the meeting and not duck off into some dark alleyway or other exit of escape. It had taken every ounce of courage I could muster to trust this process, get out of my car, and continue to follow Kim's leading. What steps of courage do you need to take?

The meeting took place at an older apartment complex that had an outside fire-escape stairwell, with steps that could be pulled down from each floor. I would be lying if I said I didn't have my eyes on those stairs—just in case. Kim kept me moving. No long explanations. No talking. No coddling or idle chatter. She knew I needed much more than talking and counseling. I needed to experience God's presence for myself, something beyond human efforts and explanations. God speaks through His people, but there comes a time in every person's life when they need to experience God personally. When the Holy Spirit is in the driver's seat, we experience the power of His presence.

REMOVING STRONGHOLDS

When Kim and I entered a one-bedroom apartment on the fifth floor, I was startled to see the living room filled with ladies, young and old. The oldest, I would later learn, was eighty-five years old. She was the matriarch of the bunch, the leading "spiritual mother" of the house. When I took in this scene, you can bet those fire-escape stairs were vivid in my mind. All I needed was an opportunity to slip out of the room, find a window, and down I could go.

My anxiety spiked. I had trouble catching my breath, and I was sweating profusely. It felt like a panic attack. My heart seemed to beat out of my chest. Meanwhile, all the other women in the room were happy, laughing, sharing with one another—and dressed quite a bit differently than me, I might add. Their cleavage was fully covered, and their jeans weren't painted onto their skin like mine were. My makeup was heavy, and my long bleach-blonde hair hung down to my backside. My belly chain had a charm hanging right above the top button on the front of my jeans. Most of my fake-tan, bronzed skin on my muscle-toned body was exposed.

The enemy's spirit of judgment came upon me, even though no one in the room condemned me. I didn't look like them, talk like them, or celebrate like they did. Words can't even describe how out of place I felt, and yet I was in the perfect place. I was exactly where God wanted me to be, exposed cleavage and all. Even while I was broken and angry at God, He still surrounded me with help, hope, and love. These women would be yet another lifeline.

But would I have the courage to surrender to God?

The eighty-five-year-old woman, whom everyone addressed as "Mama," called us all to attention. The ladies promptly responded by quieting themselves and encircling the room, with most people sitting on the floor. Seated on a small, worn loveseat, Mama rested her hands on a Bible lying on the 1970s coffee table in front of her and told us to prepare our hearts as she spoke. She delivered such an encouraging and loving message about God and how He wanted to move in our hearts. I was resistant, but my desire to know more was greater than my hesitation, doubt, and fears. I listened intently. She prayed and then asked if anyone had anything to share. The silence was deafening. No one else spoke, and there was no way I was going to share anything in this room. I didn't know these women. They seemed perfect and holy, very unlike me. I was damaged goods, promiscuous, doing things I had never thought I would do, living a life so far into darkness that I believed even God couldn't rescue me.

Then, suddenly, I did something unexpected. I raised my hand. I started sobbing, and I began spewing out confessions about every filthy part of my life, along with how I felt about the abuses, afflictions, betrayals, hurts, and harms that had been inflicted upon me. The guilt, shame, and regret that had consumed me poured out everywhere. I just couldn't stop the flow. It was as if twenty years of torment were jetting out of me. During this time of uncontrollable sobbing, I could truly feel my brokenness for the first time.

The women didn't intervene. They didn't try to console me or remove me from the moment. They knew what the Lord was doing. Finally, I had no more words. I could no longer speak. I just buried my face in my hands, sobbing wretchedly.

Then Mama told the other ladies to grab a chair from the kitchen and get ready. She walked over to me and said, "Stand up, my child. Come with me." I took her hand, and she led me over to the chair, which had been placed in the middle of the room. A handful of older women, including Kim, gathered around me while the other ladies looked on, and some prayed. Mama smeared oil on my head, and those women laid hands on me and began to pray in a language I had never heard before. My emotions vacillated between shock and awe. But there was another power in that room that was stronger than any controlled substance I had ever used. I discovered that these women were prayer warriors. This was not their first rodeo, nor was I the first woman needing deliverance who had come across their path. These were seasoned, mature women of faith who knew how to cast out and cast down the demons controlling my life. They knew the only power that could make me well was the power of God Himself flowing through every part of me.

As their voices became louder, I was still sobbing, and I grabbed onto Kim's hand, squeezing it with all my might. It felt like hot towels were being laid across my back. I actually told the ladies to stop putting towels on me. I kept saying, "They're too hot, they're too hot." Kim leaned over to me and said, "Tracy, you're okay. Just let go. Surrender. We've got you." Softly, I uttered, "I surrender." The women kept praying, and I felt a presence inside me like I had never felt before. I sensed a rushing movement through my belly and a peace that immersed every part of me. I felt as if my breath had left my body and someone else was breathing for me.

I didn't recognize it at the time, but I was receiving the supernatural power and touch of God. I did understand that something beyond human ability or explanation was taking place, even though I had never before experienced anything like it.

The women kept interceding for me. They were fervent and determined, and they forcefully prayed that God would have His will and way with my life.

> **I FELT AS IF MY BREATH HAD LEFT MY BODY AND SOMEONE ELSE WAS BREATHING FOR ME.**

After nearly half an hour of this warring prayer, an overwhelming stillness and calm came over me. My sobbing stopped. My fear left me. It felt like every bad thing had been removed from my mind and body. I felt completely drained, but I was also in an indescribable state of tranquility. I let go of Kim's hand and sat up. It wasn't until then that the ladies began to pray a little more softly. They did not remove their hands. Mama started praying in English, thanking and glorifying God for His mighty work. That night, those ladies prayed against every demon in hell that had come against me, and they were victorious. These women knew how to break off strongholds and life-controlling issues. They understood that the battles we face are beyond human initiation or consequence. They knew there was a spiritual war going on, and they knew exactly how to fight to win it.

The Bible teaches about the root causes of our spiritual struggles and strongholds, and how to overcome them:

For our struggle is not against flesh and blood [contending only with physical opponents], but against the rulers, against the powers, against the world forces of this [present] darkness, against the spiritual forces of wickedness in the heavenly (supernatural) places.

(Ephesians 6:12 AMP)

For though we walk in the flesh [as mortal men], we are not carrying on our [spiritual] warfare according to the flesh and using the weapons of man. The weapons of our warfare are not physical [weapons of flesh and blood]. Our weapons are divinely powerful for the destruction of fortresses. We are destroying sophisticated arguments and every exalted and proud thing that sets itself up against the [true] knowledge of God, and we are taking every thought and purpose captive to the obedience of Christ, being ready to punish every act of disobedience, when your own obedience [as a church] is complete.

(2 Corinthians 10:3–6 AMP)

God's Word is very clear about the spiritual battles that are continually waged within every person, whether they belong to Jesus Christ or not. We face not only attacks from Satan, but also the opposition of our sinful human nature. Without Christ and the power of the Holy Spirit, we have no power to overcome that sinful nature. Using our human reason and instinct, we think we know what's best for us, but our reason and instinct can be very flawed. The Holy Spirit, who abides with every Christian, provides the power to overcome sinful temptations, break off strongholds, and persevere in faithful obedience to God. Without the Holy Spirit, defeat reigns, and strength is an illusion. Apart from Christ, who is the Bread of Life and the Water of Life, we are starving and parched.

I needed Jesus. I needed to be saved from my sins and filled with the power of the Holy Spirit. However, although I experienced a powerful touch from God during the prayer meeting, I did not repent of my sins and receive God's gift of salvation at that time. When I had first arrived at the meeting, I was on life support, spiritually speaking. I was suffocating under the weight of the enemy's attacks. My past hurts had created spiritual strongholds within me that kept me from trusting Jesus. I had refused to run to God and therefore could not be saved. These women knew this. They knew I needed a touch from God *before* I could turn to Him and surrender my life to Him. Those strongholds of darkness needed to be demolished by the Holy Spirit before I could be rescued by God.

I praise the Lord for the obedience of those prayer warriors and for their boldness, their preparation, their knowledge of God's Word, and their sacrifices in serving the Lord. Without them, I would not have experienced the breaking of the strongholds that had held me captive for years. God used these faithful women because they believed in His power and obeyed Him. They were able, ready, and willing to be used. These women were Spirit-filled, and they spoke in "tongues," which are prayer languages that come straight from God. Tongues are used to pray beyond our human ability. It is the purity of the Holy Spirit that produces supernatural healing, transformation, and so much more. As a result of my experience in that prayer meeting, my life would be changed forever from the inside out. But it would take a while for the outward changes to manifest.

No matter what your situation is, I encourage you to keep taking the next step and allowing the Lord to change you and draw you ever closer to Himself. Although I was not yet committed to Christ, when I left that prayer meeting, I was filled with a hunger and a thirst to pursue God. I pray that you will become filled with the same hunger and thirst to go after God with everything in you. Amazingly, a woman who had practically hated God and cringed at the name of Jesus was suddenly on fire to learn about the Lord. My problems and struggles did not instantly fall away, but I now had the courage and resolve to face them. I no longer wanted to throw my life away. Something had happened inside me, and I wanted to know what it was and how I could make it last.

I later learned that every woman in that prayer meeting had experienced a similar move of God in their life. Before they were saved and changed by the power of God, they were in circumstances similar to my own. I will be eternally grateful for this remnant of women who believed that God's power, delivered through the Holy Spirit, could transform my life. If only we would truly trust God's way of doing things! Our world needs to experience a fresh movement of the Holy Spirit and His wondrous power.

ACCOUNTABILITY AND DISCIPLESHIP

After that prayer meeting, Kim instructed me to call her every morning at 8:00 sharp. She warned me that all hell was about to break loose in my life and that I needed an accountability partner. She wasn't exaggerating. Spiritual warfare had begun. The enemy did not want me to receive God's healing and be transformed. Likewise, he does not want you to be free and filled with faith and the power of God.

Satan wants you stuck, held captive, rendered useless and powerless. He wants you as far away from following Jesus as he can get you. He will oppose your victories in Christ and the steps you take toward breakthrough. The enemy will try to prevent you from attending church weekly, reading your Bible daily, singing worship songs, and fellowshipping with other Christians. It's his master plan. He knows these spiritual practices make you strong and victorious. He knows that if you follow them, he will lose the death grip he has on you to hold you hostage and stifle your life. Always be mindful of his schemes, but also know that God is greater and stronger than the devil and any demon from hell. When Jesus died on the cross, He defeated Satan. Since the enemy has already been defeated, he is powerless to control you as long as your life is active in Christ and on freedom's pathway.

I started to learn about the Holy Spirit from Kim, a true woman of God. She taught me with great patience, leading me into the spiritual steps needed to fully break off crippling strongholds and every form of darkness and prevent them from returning. She taught me how to not just read the Bible but also study it and apply the Scriptures to my daily living. She would repeatedly say to me, "Tracy, keep learning about and surrendering to the Holy Spirit, and He will set you free of every spiritual bondage." Kim wasn't exaggerating. She was teaching me discipline and how to develop a godly routine in my life. This whole process through which Kim was patiently taking me is called *discipleship*, friend! Without it, you cannot heal and become the new creation that God is calling you to be.

Kim led a Bible study in her home every Wednesday night at seven. It was a good thing it was in her home, because I still wasn't ready to set foot in a church. I didn't feel worthy or think I would be accepted by church-going folks. I am grateful God called Kim to this Bible-study ministry and for her obedience to His call. She was leading many women just like me into church through the back door. Kim opened the doors to her home, which, over time, led us through the doors of the churches we ultimately attended and joined.

Women from every walk of life showed up at her Bible study. If they didn't have a babysitter, Kim told them to bring their kids with them. Her bedroom became my children's playroom. Although Kim only had a one-bedroom apartment, she didn't let that stop her from hosting fifteen women at a time. Inside her tiny home, she poured her life into mine and others, and God showed up. (Do you know someone who needs you to be the church for them before inviting them to church?)

DAY OF SURRENDER TO GOD

One morning, I couldn't get Kim's voice out of my head. After I'd had multiple discussions with her regarding my anger toward God, she had instructed me to cry out to Him and ask Him to forgive me—when I felt ready to do so. I asked how I would know when the time was right. She simply said, "You will no longer be able to fight the overwhelming feelings. They will consume and pester you until you surrender. This is God's way of showing you your need to let go of your anger and allow Him to help, heal, and love you." And she regularly told me, "Give your struggles over at the same time you give Him your life. Give Him your anger; He can handle it." Kim's words reverberated in my ears. However, my Catholic upbringing had taught me that I dared not be angry with God or question His authority. I reasoned that since God is holy, He wouldn't save a woman like me. Ever since I had been molested by my neighbor when I was eight years old, I had felt unsafe and unworthy of God's love. Neither did I believe He could possibly love me if He had allowed that to happen in the first place.

However, on that particular morning, my bitterness toward God erupted like a volcano. I wept for what seemed like several hours as I vented my anger at Him. "Why didn't You save me? Why didn't You rescue me? Why did You let that man molest me? Why did You let those men rape me when I was enslaved to my addiction? Why did You let my life turn out like this? Why, God? Why weren't You there? Why didn't You show up for me? Why?"

Amazingly, in the midst of my ranting, I felt God's overwhelming love for me. I experienced a powerful peace within me and a sense of safety in His presence. It felt as if God was fighting for me as I rested in His arms. And that's when I finally let go of all my anger toward Him, asked for His forgiveness, and professed Jesus as my Savior and Lord. Emotionally and physically spent, I cried myself to sleep. I knew I had just experienced another life-changing moment. There was no turning back. Ever since that prayer meeting in the fifth-floor apartment, I had been seeking God, but this was the beginning of my journey with His Son, Jesus Christ. It had taken me baby steps to get there, but, one day at a time, one powerful choice at a time, I had finally surrendered my life to Christ completely.

The next day, I immediately shared my experience with Kim. She asked me what I thought about attending church services. When I hesitated slightly, she boldly jumped in and said, "Tracy, it's time." I knew she was right. I trusted her. The next step of the healing process was before me. It was time to muster up the courage to attend church.

With Kim's assistance, I looked up various churches in my area and found a Bible-based congregation that I chose to attend. I was still very rough around the edges, and God was working on the inside of me as well as on the outside. Still clothed in my skimpy attire, I made the choice to walk through the doors of the Church of All Nations in Boca Raton, Florida. At the end of the worship service, I responded to Pastor Mark Boykin's invitation by walking down the center aisle to the altar and publicly professing my faith in Christ. As I mentioned earlier, I had walked church aisles in years past when I was younger, only to continue living in sin, still enslaved to the desires of addiction, with no power to refuse the calls of darkness when they rang. Again, I had thought that God didn't save people like me who had fallen so far from His grace. But I couldn't have been more wrong.

My previous church altar experiences had been nothing more than emotional attempts to manipulate God into bailing me out of dire situations. I thank God for churches where they take you aside after you make the most important decision of your life, and they explain what has just transpired: a divine exchange that takes a lifetime to experience. At Church of all Nations, I was immediately connected with a woman who explained the implications of my decision to publicly profess Jesus Christ as my Savior and Lord. During our conversation, she emphasized how vital it was for me to be discipled. Discipleship simply means learning the ways of God with a person who can lead you into an understanding of the Word of God and the foundations of faith in Christ. Thanks to Kim and her Bible studies, I was already familiar with the process. God was surrounding me with Jesus-loving, God-fearing, and Bible-living women who would teach me, lead me, and love me right into that very same life in Christ.

Ladies, have you invited God-fearing women to speak God's truth and grace into your life? Gentlemen, have you invited God-fearing men to help lead, guide, and grow you in the ways of Christ? Are you being discipled in the Word of God? I'm not talking about attending church, visiting God's Word every now and then, reading a five-minute devotional here and there, or skimming through an article about a biblical topic through an app on your mobile device. I'm talking about going deep with God by means of intentional personal Bible study and life application through weekly discipleship and fellowship with other Christians. The deeper you go with God, friend, the greater your freedom will be as you allow Jesus to be in the driver's seat of your life. His ways are powerful, filled with favor and open doors you could never manufacture on your own. Jesus is your everything. And He's waiting for you.

> **THE DEEPER YOU GO WITH GOD, FRIEND, THE GREATER YOUR FREEDOM WILL BE AS YOU ALLOW JESUS TO BE IN THE DRIVER'S SEAT OF YOUR LIFE.**

SERVING THE PURPOSES OF GOD

After my salvation experience, I wanted everyone I knew to profess their faith in Jesus. I became like a "mini Kim," loving multitudes of broken women right into prayer meetings, then right into the front doors of my church. These women had recognized I was changing and heard the excitement in my voice as I talked practically all the time about Jesus without using those colorful, four-letter words I was infamous for saying. To them, I was a walking, talking miracle.

I would show up in the church parking lot with my SUV filled with women from my recovery meetings. My green Ford Explorer was like a circus clown car when we arrived at church, as the women just kept pouring out of my vehicle. All of us, of course, had to smoke one final cigarette in the parking lot before going into the building. The girls and I would stamp out our cigarettes and place them in a Ziploc bag that I kept in my purse. I wasn't about to let the ladies litter the parking lot of the house of God with nasty cigarette butts! Pretty holy, right? Remember, salvation is immediate, but sanctification—the process of becoming more like Christ—is progressive. And, praise God, Jesus doesn't ask you to clean up before you come to Him. You come to Jesus so *He* can do the forgiving, cleaning, healing, and transforming.

Those ladies and I would then walk into the church, skimpy clothes and all. God would later change our appearance too. He knew we didn't yet know our value or worth, but, in time, the love of God transformed us. We covered our cleavages, wore our skirts longer and longer, and eventually gave up our cigarettes. I was far from perfect, but God was working in me and through me to rescue His daughters from torment and the pit of hell through His great love. I didn't know the Bible yet, but I knew the preacher did. I knew where to take the women, and I used my SUV as the means to get them there.

STAYING CLOSE TO GOD

What are you waiting for, friend? If I could invite carloads of women to church while barely knowing how to pray or what the Bible teaches, you can too. Who can you invite or take to church? How does God want to use you? Who do you know that needs a touch from God? Or perhaps you are the one in need of a touch. Are you like I was, hurt and angry at God, running away from church, living a destructive lifestyle? Your life is too important—*you* are too important—for you to continue living the way you have been.

Don't let the devil or a hurt from a past experience keep you out of church and away from God and your destiny. Come home to your heavenly Father. If you've never been to church, and you're pondering the thought of attending a congregation for the first time, think no more. Make the choice to find a scripturally solid church that teaches the Bible and believes in the transforming work of the Holy Spirit. Get inside those church doors and experience the power of God that awaits you. Your life will never be the same.

If you've been a churchgoer for a while, perhaps you are experiencing a difficult season in life, or maybe you feel stagnant or empty. I have been in that place more than once, and I know I will be there again sometime. But I know what to do during those seasons of spiritual drought. I persevere in my relationship with God. I encourage you to walk into the next service at your home church with determination. Don't forsake assembling together with your fellow Christians for worship and Bible study. (See Hebrews 10:25.) I bring a notebook and pen and write down every word that grabs my attention as the pastor or Bible study leader teaches. And even if it doesn't speak strongly to me at the time, I write down every Scripture reference mentioned, and I later read those Scriptures along with the entire chapter of the Bible in which they are found.

In my quiet time at home, during which I spend time with God, praying and reading the Bible, I ask the Father to reveal Himself to me in a fresh way. I ask the Holy Spirit to overtake every part of my life and to move within me. Sometimes I experience the Spirit's move immediately; in other seasons, it takes longer. For a fresh perspective, I also read different translations of the Bible that seem to particularly awaken my spirit. I will often set aside time to go somewhere outside of my home—such as a park or, if it's raining, a mall—to pray and read the Bible, just to alter my routine. I become laser-focused on gratitude, and I thank God for every little thing, even if my world is falling apart.

You will be amazed at how quickly such practices will change your countenance and improve your outlook on life. Friend, do not forget that our God is always faithful. You will feel Him, experience Him, and hear Him once again. And, during those times when you don't sense Him, know that He is always working for your good and His glory. Persevere! You are worth it.

Today, I am a mighty woman of God whose goal is to win as many souls for Jesus as I can for His glory. My husband, Darryl, and I hold positions on the executive board of our current home church, Journey Church, in Troy, Missouri, with Senior Pastors Jesse and Missy Quiroz. They, too, understand how vital discipleship is. Every Sunday, people are invited and challenged to know Christ, to grow in Christ, or to receive prayer for other needs. The altar is lined with men and women of God who are equipped and ready to welcome all those who come forward for prayer and discipleship.

I can't underscore enough that we must grow in the knowledge and ways of God to experience fullness of life in Him. This is a lifelong journey in which we can experience God's best as we increasingly entrust our lives to Him. Choose to let go and let God. Give every part of your life to Him, and allow the healing to flow!

COURAGE CHOICES FOR YOUR HEALING

1. Reread the following excerpt from the end of the section entitled "Look for the People God Sends Your Way." Then begin to write freely and with great honesty as you answer the questions.

> What's your situation, friend? What's holding you back? What's tempting you to remain stuck or to quit on yourself and your life? Perhaps you can't relate to being a slave to raging addictions. But let me ask you: where does God need to release the pressure that is smothering you? Do you long to take a deep breath followed by a soul-cleansing exhalation that discharges the stress and anxiety emanating from your core? How long have you been stuck, broken, or frustrated? Bound to life-controlling issues or self-destructive patterns? Held captive to a loved one who doesn't want to be well or change their ways?

Acknowledge your situation and then say a simple prayer of surrender to God. Here is a sample prayer of surrender:

> Father, I release every part of me, every aspect of my life, and all that I am going through. I acknowledge that I need You. Holy Spirit, I invite You into my life right now to help, lead, guide, and heal me. Thank You for giving me the courage to walk out this healing journey. Continue to work in my life. I trust You, Lord. In Jesus's name I pray, amen.

2. Are you struggling with a "Why, God?" moment or area of your life, such as I described in the section "Day of Surrender to God"?

> Why didn't You save me? Why didn't You rescue me? Why did You let that man molest me? Why did You let those men rape me when I was enslaved to my addiction? Why did You let my life turn out like this? Why, God? Why weren't You there? Why didn't You show up for me? Why?

What are your own "Why?" questions? Are you ready to surrender one or all of them to God so He can heal you? God will not move in your life until you give Him permission to work. Remember, He is a gentleman and waits patiently for us. It's time, friend. Surrender, and then surrender again. Pray the above prayer of surrender from question 1 once more, realizing that surrender is a lifelong process.

3. List one step you must take toward your breakthrough—only one for now. If you are struggling over which one to list, write down the first one that comes to mind.

4. Are you ready to move into your God-given purpose, or do you need a touch from God? Answer the following questions from the section "Staying Close to God":

    +   Who can you invite or take to church?

    +   How does God want to use you?

    +   Do you know someone who needs a touch from God?

    +   Are you the one who is in need of a touch?

    +   Are you like I was, hurt and angry at God, running away from church, living a destructive lifestyle? Your life is too important—*you* are too important—for you to continue living the way you have been. If you're not already attending a church, I encourage you to find a Bible-teaching church in your area and begin attending. Sometimes it takes several visits to a few churches to know where the Holy Spirit is leading you. The church will begin to feel like home. List the names of a few churches and then begin to visit them. Get going, friend! It's time!

5. Life transformation—God's way. Answer these questions from the section "Day of Surrender to God":

   + Ladies, have you invited God-fearing women to speak God's truth and grace into your life?

   + Gentlemen, have you invited God-fearing men to help lead, guide, and grow you in the ways of Christ?

   + Are you being discipled in the Word of God?

   If your answer to these questions is no, ask your pastor or another trusted Christian leader how to get started in a discipleship program/process.

3

LOVE'S COUNTERFEIT, AND ITS CURE

As the song asks, "What's love got to do with it?" My answer: everything! *Love* is a very small word, but it has a profound depth of meaning that we will be exploring throughout this chapter. The main purpose of our hearts, in both a spiritual and an emotional sense, is to give and receive love. Therefore, our concept of love and our capacity to give and receive love have huge ramifications in our lives. If we have a distorted view of love or a false concept of how love is expressed, we will find ourselves struggling with disabling habits and suffering one painful experience after another in our relationships.

That was certainly the case for me. All my life, I had desperately wanted to experience love in a deep way. Yet equally as destructive as my addictions was my inability to love or be loved. I chased my addictions with a fury, and I pursued love in the same manner. I longed for the happily-ever-after fairy tale. Although my parents loved me dearly, somehow, something was always missing in my heart. In response, I developed what is known as codependency.

WHAT IS CODEPENDENCY?

An individual with codependency has a need to "rescue" others. Codependency is a fear-based condition that resides deep within a person, demanding that its own needs be met in unhealthy ways. This condition stems from many root causes, such as the experience of rejection, not being loved or feeling loved, low self-esteem, lack of self-worth, fear of being alone, or anxiety over experiencing painful consequences due to another person's negative behavior.

A person with codependency will strive to clean up and cover up the emotional, psychological, physical, financial, legal, or other consequences in another person's life in hopes that the other person will change their behavior, thus becoming someone who will make them feel safe, secure, and happy. Their hope of living a successful life, one in which they are content and free, is dependent upon the life and behavior of the other person instead of on themselves. Thus, codependency is revealed by an individual's unhealthy facilitating of another person's behavior, justification for their rescuing activities, and negative emotional responses when the change they expected in the other person is not realized. Someone with codependency requires their own deep healing journey, with a focus on personal life transformation, not the other person's need to change.

Like denial, codependency is a silent killer. It masks itself as love, faithfulness, and loyalty, but, in reality, it enables the person who needs to change to continue in their destructive or stagnant behavior. It leaves the enabler exhausted physically, emotionally, and/or financially, without seeing any lasting change for the better. Meanwhile, the enabler's own life becomes lost as their life is consumed trying to manage the conduct of the other person.

Friend, you cannot change another person, no matter how hard you try, how deeply you love, or how enticing you make the desired change seem. But the freeing news is that you can decide to change *yourself* and the trajectory of your own life. People change only when they decide to do so. In making that statement, I'm not just referring to your lost loved one, but to you, as well, my friend! Remember, we experience lasting life transformation by receiving the power of God, submitting to the process of change, and partnering with God to fulfill our life's destiny. Then we will truly be transformed in our thinking and behavior, experiencing life-changing results!

TRAPPED IN A CODEPENDENT LIFESTYLE

Because of my codependency and other issues, a cycle of dysfunctional loving became a life pattern for me. Over the years, it greatly tore down my self-esteem and caused me tremendous heartache. I had a bad habit of losing myself in relationships. I guess you could say that my "picker" was defective. I always seemed to choose as my significant other someone who needed to be propped up or fixed. If I didn't choose him, I allowed him to choose me. Instead of running from all the relational red flags, I would gather every one of them and map out a plan for how I was going to save the relationship.

According to the reasoning of my savior complex, my partner should love me even more for not bailing on the relationship when I had every reason to do so. If I tolerated my partner's toxic behavior and betrayal, I would eventually win his unyielding loyalty and love. Surely, my faithfulness would conquer my partner's unfaithfulness. All of my efforts would make up for my partner's lack of effort to make the relationship work. Then I could be loved the way I needed and deserved to be loved. After all, I'd sacrificed and invested way too much of my life into the relationship to call it quits now. I'd lost too much time, passed over too many other opportunities, and forfeited my joy for far too long to give up. And, surely, my partner deserved one more chance to prove how sorry he really was. Right?

I wince as I recall all the dumpster-fire relationships I endured. There's nothing more painful than loving somebody who cannot or will not love you back. I would give my everything, only to receive almost nothing in return. I would lose myself wishing and waiting for my partner to find himself. The problem is, I was always working harder to change the other person's behavior or lifestyle than he was. These are all signs and behaviors of an individual who struggles with codependency, and my case was severe. At the time, I was familiar with the term *codependency* but not its definition or how it played out in a person's life.

LIKE DENIAL, CODEPENDENCY IS A SILENT KILLER. IT MASKS ITSELF AS LOVE, FAITHFULNESS, AND LOYALTY, BUT, IN REALITY, IT ENABLES THE PERSON WHO NEEDS TO CHANGE TO CONTINUE IN THEIR DESTRUCTIVE OR STAGNANT BEHAVIOR.

ANSWERING THE "WHY'S"

Before I met my husband, Darryl, I was divorced twice and had a string of unhealthy relationships. I dated various men of different nationalities, but, truth be told, they were all the same on the inside. Externally, they were always good-looking and exciting; yet, internally, they were incapable of healthy loving and living. I'm not judging them at all. I used to blame each one of them and loathe them in my self-pity, feeling that I was the victim of yet another failed relationship. I was always casting blame outward instead of looking inward. The painful truth is that I was the only common denominator in all those unions.

In a process I will describe shortly, I had to take a hard look at myself if I wanted to be well. I had to ask myself a few tough questions:

+ Why did I choose these partners?

+ Why did I allow them to pick me?

+ When things started to go very wrong in the relationships, why did I stay?

+ Why did I marry partners in the midst of their mess, their empty promises, and their inability to truly love me?

I had the choice to decline their advances, and yet I chose not to. I had the option to leave at the beginning of the relationships when the "deal-breaking" behaviors were taking place, but I didn't.

If you are in a similar situation, it's crucial for you to take the time to answer the above questions as well. If you're already married and not just dating, then you are now in a covenantal relationship ordained by God that is not to be easily broken. If your marriage seems hopeless, divorce does not have to be your only option. My husband and I have written a book entitled *The Imperfect Marriage: Help for Those Who Think It's Over*, in which we explain how marriage reconciliation is possible. (However, if you are experiencing physical or emotional abuse, you need to protect yourself and immediately consult a trusted and trained counselor.)[3]

I have learned this crucial truth over the years: your own inner brokenness will draw you into dysfunctional relationships with unhealthy

---

3. Within the United States, you can search for local assistance online by going to the website of The National Resource Center on Domestic Violence at https://nrcdv.org.

partners. These relationships are a by-product of two unhealed hearts within the people who are trying to love one another. Usually, one person is the extreme giver, and the other is the extreme taker. Both parties have emotional wounds that produce toxic relationships. If you suffer from codependency—knowingly or unknowingly—you will be drawn to people who need to be fixed, and these relationships will break your heart every time. Again, in codependent relationships, the "fixer" carries the heavy load, all the while hoping for the day their "taker" will finally be part of the solution. Yet that day never comes.

POTENTIAL IS NOT REALITY

If "love is blind," then codependency is delusional. I would fall in love with my partner's potential while dreaming of love and ignoring reality. Potential is a dangerous characteristic to fall in love with. You have the ability to see who a person *can be* or *what they can become*, and yet they are not that person. Potential is a position of hope of what might be, not what really is. An outlook of envisioning what might be can be helpful in some areas of life, such as following a goal for your life, but the sort of hoping I am referring to here is fruitless in codependent relationships. Before long, you're in love with the dream, and you continue to ignore the reality. People fall in love with potential every day. As I did, many of them will take their false dream right down the aisle into the sacred covenant of marriage. But, then, the "I do's" quickly become undone because they were never possible to achieve in the first place.

I actually participated in such unrealistic matrimonial unions on three separate occasions. Darryl and I are both in our third marriage. When we married, we were headed down the same dead-end road through the identical dysfunctional pattern of loving. It was another setup for heartbreak. And heartbreak it was, until I found the courage to heal and stand my ground. As in my previous relationships, I had fallen in love with Darryl's potential. There were two sides to his personality. At times, I could see the depths of his greatness; but then the other side of him would appear through destructive behaviors that would shred my heart to pieces.

I had behaved in the same way before I experienced God's healing power, which made me whole and changed me forever. My children and anyone else who had tried to love me, including my ex-husbands, other family members, and friends, had experienced this double personality in their relationships with me. They would see glimpses of the real Tracy, whom God had created me to be, but then they would witness the emergence of the destructive, unhealed Tracy who was broken and lost. I desired to genuinely love others, but I was not able to do so in a stable, consistent, healthy way. I have to be honest: I did not know the true meaning of love. It took me a long time to discover true love in God through Christ.

Counterfeit love poisons every aspect of our lives. There is a reason people get lost in dysfunction, and an unhealed heart is the main culprit. When your heart is broken, love is shattered. A broken heart, emotional and physical wounds, and betrayals from childhood through adulthood contaminate true love.

For years, therefore, my inability to love and be loved brought me—and others—great pain, confusion, and emptiness in multiple failed relationships. Many times, I entered a downward spiral that led to loss, division, separation from loved ones, and divorce. I looked for love in all the wrong places. All I found was lust for sensual pleasures, meaningless pledges of fidelity, and conditional expressions of endearment. Frankly, I didn't love who I was, and I couldn't love others simply for who they were. Have you ever heard that expression "You can't love others if you don't love yourself"? That statement is so true, friend, and that was my truth for a long time. Not loving myself meant I allowed others to trespass healthy boundaries in my life, mainly because I had yet to define and establish for myself a right standard of value and self-worth.

HAVING HIGH STANDARDS OF LIVING AND LOVING

Individuals who are emotionally heart-healthy adopt high standards of living and loving to which they remain faithful. Those standards are evidence of operational safeguards in their lives that maintain their emotional health and enable them to love in the wholesome way God intended. With such safeguards in place, their internal sense of strength, value, and worth will not accept continual, painful trespasses from others with whom they are in relationship. They recognize and reject entering into a relationship with someone whose actions threaten the sanctity of their well-being and that of those around them. They will no longer tolerate the intolerable or accept the unacceptable. They will refuse to lose themselves while trying to love another person. They know that only Jesus can save a lost soul, heal a broken heart, and change a life, including their own.

By experiencing the healing power of Jesus, we can embrace a new identity in Him, rising above settling for anything less than God's best. The reason I tried to find love by desperately pursuing romantic relationships was that I didn't love myself or understand God's love. I thought those relationships would bring me happiness, success, acceptance, and validation. I kept hoping that, someday, love would win the day, week, month, and year so I could finally break that vicious cycle of toxic, failed relationships. But I kept chasing love's counterfeit. Eventually, I learned that when you bring unhealed wounds into a relationship, you sabotage your chances of success. Out of a damaged heart come selfishness that crowds out selflessness, recurring arguments that are never resolved, and outbursts of anger that erupt without provocation. Adulteries, addictions, passivity, simply checking out of the relationship, and so many other forms of destructive behavior spread like wildfire. Lifeless days become the norm.

Another detriment of my codependency was that my personal growth and achievements were stalled. Life continued to pass me by as I obsessively focused my time, attention, and energy on saving my partner from the consequences of his mistakes, or simply waited in vain for my partner to love me back and change his destructive lifestyle. Notice that word *waited*? I waited for him. I waited for everyone and everything else around me to change until, eventually, I looked inward, became honest with myself, and realized that I was the one who needed to change if my life was going to be changed for the better. I recognized that I was responsible for my own happiness and freedom. I was responsible for pursuing the dreams and legacy of my life. There was to be no more waiting for others to complete me.

I assure you, what you refuse to conquer will conquer you. However, what you face head-on, you can overcome through the power of God and the process of change. Husband number three is what it took for me to realize this painful but freeing revelation.

*WHAT YOU REFUSE TO CONQUER WILL CONQUER YOU.
HOWEVER, WHAT YOU FACE HEAD-ON, YOU CAN OVERCOME
THROUGH THE POWER OF GOD AND THE PROCESS OF CHANGE.*

WHEN DARRYL CAME INTO MY LIFE

The first time I met Darryl, he was the sweetest man. I encountered the side of him that God had created him to be: genuinely caring, gentle, and loving. We were introduced at a recovery convention. I had been clean and sober for one year, while Darryl had just about three hours under his belt. His friends had picked him up from a dangerous drug binge and brought him to the convention. There he was, this famous former Major League Baseball player known for his power at the plate and speed around the bases. He had built a legacy that is cherished by fans around the world to this day. Darryl was known as one of the best players in the world, and yet now he was struggling just to stay alive. On the night we met, he was genuinely fighting for his life.

I watched from across the room as his fans surrounded him like piranhas, competing for their window of opportunity for a picture and an autograph from their baseball great. "What is wrong with everybody?" I asked in an intentionally loud voice to a friend who was seated next to me. I was sickened and saddened by this repulsive behavior. It was as if no one saw Darryl as a person, the suffering soul that he was. They just kept exploiting a man who had no life left in him.

Peace and happiness cannot be purchased. Darryl's money couldn't change him, and his fame couldn't save him. He had lost everything, including the ability to be loved as a person simply for the man he was, and not for his achievements on the baseball field. It broke my heart to see people take advantage of him. He had such a gentle look and way about him. He was so kind and tolerated every moment of that freak show with his fans, which continued for hours.

Darryl was seated in a high-back chair that seemed to prop up his emaciated frame, which was too frail to support itself. The evidence of his addiction was shocking and heartbreaking. This formerly muscular power-house of a hitter looked as if he barely weighed a hundred pounds soaking wet. His face was drawn, his clothes were excessively baggy because he had lost so much weight, and there was a yellowing in his eyes that revealed the depth of his story of decline. His addictions were killing him—and most people didn't seem to care.

What I was witnessing was so disturbing to me that I felt I had to get out of that meeting. Seated beside Darryl were Chris and Carolyn, a married couple who were dear friends of mine, and who I noticed were apparently good friends of Darryl as well. I had driven Chris, Carolyn, and a few others to the convention that evening, and Chris was holding my car keys in his pocket. When I approached Chris to get my keys, he stood up and said, "I want you to meet my friend Darryl."

"Nice to meet you," I quickly replied and turned back to Chris with my palm held out for my keys, which he slowly placed in my hand. At that moment, Darryl held on tightly to the arms of his high-back chair and slowly stood up. He reached out his hand to gently embrace my arm and commented, "Leaving so soon? Would you stay a while longer?"

Seeing those soft, kind eyes, yellow or not, it was easy to oblige. That evening, I experienced Darryl's loving heart and gentle soul in the few hours we spent talking about our struggles and pain. Baseball was never the topic, nor did I care for it to be. I cared about this man's soul and the destiny of his life. We were two broken souls longing to be accepted and loved, desperately desiring to be healed, whole, and well. Yet we were far from the realization of those desires.

Inexplicably, we quickly fell for each other. But let me tell you, friend, desire is not enough! God put the desire to love and be loved in the heart of every person. The key is, He also designed the way to successful loving: having a strong, healthy, emotional heart and godly character. This makes a person *able* to love. A desire to be wanted, needed, and loved can drive us hard from within. That desire will hurt us every time if it is not accompanied by an understanding of the true nature of love and the *ability* to love. I kept ending up in romantic relationships because of my strong desire for love, but those relationships ended in disaster because of my (and often my partners') lack of ability to make love work.

Our brokenness, desire for love, and relatability brought Darryl and me together, but it would later tear us apart. We were filled with potential and the possibilities of a bright future. We were enthralled and intrigued with the idea of love while foolishly thinking we could make each other well and fill the parts of our souls that were empty.

Our story is really one of "lost" at first sight, not love at first sight. As I mentioned, I had been sober for only one year. Additionally, I had given my life to Christ only one week earlier. My relationship with Jesus was brand-new. I was just beginning to learn what it meant to be a Christian and how to achieve wholeness. Remember those Wednesday-night Bible studies I attended at Kim's house? I met Darryl during that time period. I was finding my way with Jesus, but I was not yet spiritually and emotionally well. My old patterns of dysfunctional loving and living were very much alive, and my heart wounds were not yet healed.

Feelings of wanting to be needed and loved overwhelmed me. They did not ask permission or come in slowly from a protected or safeguarded place. They rushed in with great force, like the waters gushing down Niagara Falls. I began glamorizing the potential for true love with Darryl and pushed away the present realities. I thought Darryl could complete me, and I would help him make up for his deficiencies. We were just what each other needed to become well, I reasoned. We could make it work. It would be different this time. Love was going to be enough. It was going to remedy every problem and withstand every storm. Love would pay the bills, heal our wounds, change our character, forgive our sins, and make all things new. Right? Wrong!

LIVING IN FRANTIC "RESCUE MODE"

With our unhealed hearts, Darryl and I plunged right into a relationship like two damaged ships on a collision course. We didn't see each other much at first, nor did we officially date because Darryl was still struggling to stay clean and sober. I was content to be his remedy, his saving grace. We would wallow in this tumultuous pursuit for about three years. I would lose sleep worrying about where he was and the condition he was in, search for him relentlessly, and pull him out of crack houses. I would physically fight anyone who stepped in my way during those daring and foolish rescues.

Placing my own life and recovery process in jeopardy, I went too far. Again, not listening to wisdom and instruction, I forged forward in my stubborn and reckless ways. I foolishly went alone on three separate occasions to rescue Darryl from drug houses.

One afternoon, I kicked open a door of a drug house where I knew Darryl had relapsed into his old ways. Right in front of me was a table filled with every type of illegal drug you could imagine. I froze in place, fixed my eyes on those party pleasures, and stared way too long. As the temptation to partake in this party intensified, I realized I had broken all the rules. I had sacrificed my safety trying to save someone who still didn't want to be saved. Darryl wasn't willing to receive hope and help and take the necessary steps to change. By the grace of God, I ran past that table, pulled Darryl out of yet another strange bed, and dragged him to the car. I was in rescue mode, and, once again, I was leaving myself, my goals, my dreams, and my life behind.

Does the description of my behavior sound familiar to you? Again, you may or may not be dealing with an addiction situation, but where have you broken the rules of engagement in the relationship arena? When, where, and how have you sacrificed your life, your dreams, your progress, your everything for someone who refuses to get well or love you the right way? How long will you continue to carry or drag the weight of another person before cutting the ties to set yourself free?

In my situation, because I didn't want to cut ties with Darryl, I kept on going until I had nothing left. Darryl had actually told me from the beginning that if I dared to love him, he was going to take me through it. And take me through it he did. But I want to make one thing clear: I was never a victim; I was a volunteer. I couldn't blame Darryl. Of course, he had to take ownership of his own life and decisions, but I had to take ownership of mine. I could have and should have walked away early in our relationship, giving God room to work and have the final say. Darryl was not my problem to fix, and loving him was not going to fix me either. God wanted my life as well. He wanted me to be whole and to get busy living out His plan for me. It was a tough lesson to learn and, at the time, an unbearable truth to accept. It took three years for me to finally be strong enough in my faith to take a stand for myself and let God have His way with both Darryl and me. The following is what transpired for me to make the necessary changes.

TAKING A STAND FOR CHRIST AND SELF-WORTH

After I lost custody of my sons, I moved from Florida back home to Missouri to live with my parents. And guess who I brought with me? You got it: Darryl. The relocation put a lot of distance between Darryl and those drug houses I was dragging him out of in Florida. But shacking up with my boyfriend under my parents' roof was not going well. The Holy Spirit was increasingly convicting me that our relationship wasn't honoring to God. One day, when I walked into the bedroom where Darryl was sleeping—the same bedroom I'd had when I was in high school—I suddenly reached the tipping point and decided that our relationship had to change.

Excitedly, I roused Darryl from his slumber and told him that we would no longer be sleeping together as an unmarried couple. I took a firm stand for Christ and my self-worth. I was no longer going to compromise my convictions and continue living in sin. To my surprise and disappointment, Darryl was not on board. But when he suggested that he probably should move out, my response was unwavering. "Yeah, I guess you better," I replied. "You know, let me help you pack."

Heartbroken, I quickly purchased a plane ticket online for him to go stay with his godparents in California. As I drove him to the airport, we barely spoke. Within just a few hours of my pledge of abstinence, Darryl was gone from my life. Sometimes, making the right decision does not always immediately result in your desired outcome, and, at other times, it does not occur at all. I've had it happen both ways, but I've never regretted taking the proper stand.

This time, it would pay off big in the long run. Whether or not Darryl and I ended up together, I knew I was doing the right thing by obeying the prompting of the Holy Spirit. If I was going to find both myself and true love, it was going to be in God's way, not mine. No longer was I going to put my life on hold in order to try to fix someone else's life in hopes of garnering his love and fidelity and securing my own happiness. I needed to focus on God's restoration plan for my life.

LETTING GO AND LETTING GOD

When I finally let go of Darryl and let God have control of our relationship, we both began to change for the better. Getting out of our own way was key to giving God space to work in our lives. As two vessels surrendered to the Lord, we had to rely on God instead of on each other. Over the next nine months, Darryl filled himself with God's Word. In the meantime, I took my life back while waiting for my relationship miracle to occur. I focused on pursuing a career in real estate and regaining my financial independence, all the while growing in my relationship with Christ and pursuing His healing. I attended every Bible study and church service I could squeeze into my schedule. I faithfully attended my Christ-centered recovery support group and enrolled in some college courses. I began to thrive as my relationship with Jesus flourished and my heart was being healed. I started to participate in my own life once again. I reengaged with healthy friends and spent quality time with my family, building memories and having fun! I took my power and destiny back, friend, and so can you!

When Darryl called me on the phone to talk about his own growing relationship with Jesus, the hope and new life in his voice were undeniable. After our nearly yearlong separation, Darryl and I were ready to unite in Christian marriage, and we said our "I do's" at A Little White Wedding Chapel in Las Vegas. See how God works? When I finally decided to get out of the way and stop trying to fix Darryl, God did what only He can do, and the Holy Spirit drew Darryl to Himself in repentance and faith. Again, the point is, I had to let go and let God. I had to get out of Darryl's way so he could run to God and not to me for saving and healing. And I had to come to the end of myself so that God could rescue, redeem, and restore my own life, with or without Darryl.

At first, my heart was crushed because it felt like the three years of selflessness and sacrifice that I had poured into Darryl's life trying to help him conquer his addictions had all been in vain. But as I grew in Christ, it was His power that gave me the courage to stop enabling Darryl's destructive lifestyle as well as my own. I still needed a lot of deep heart work to become whole once again. But, thank God, He alone is the remedy for our deepest and darkest hurts that need to be healed. He is a good God with great plans for us. God is faithful, and He will restore you too. Trust the process. Let go and let God.

GOD ALONE IS THE REMEDY FOR OUR DEEPEST AND DARKEST HURTS THAT NEED TO BE HEALED. HE IS A GOOD GOD WITH GREAT PLANS FOR US.

THE HEART OF THE MATTER

You see, friend, Darryl wasn't a bad person. He was a sick, unhealed person who needed to get well. I was not a bad person. I just needed healing and change. He and I needed the same thing, but we were going about getting it in the wrong way. We were both hurting, and hurting people hurt other people. An unhealed, hurting heart is a desperate and dangerous heart. It produces painful consequences for all those involved.

From a spiritual perspective, as well as a physical one, the heart is the most important organ we have. A whole heart has the capability to love and to be loved, to act in the right way and to live in the right way. Yet when unhealed hurts are imbedded in our hearts, we cannot function in the way God intended. As a result, we inevitably harm ourselves and others. Our unhealed hurts will wreak havoc and produce even more pain and toxic emotions, such as anger, rage, resentment, depression, lack of motivation, and other attitudes that can leave us debilitated or experiencing feelings of despair. If we have a heart that is starved for or void of God's love, it is impossible for us to love ourselves and others.

An unhealed heart is therefore toxic and dangerous. In Jeremiah 17:9, the Bible describes an unhealed heart as untrustworthy; it is *"deceitful"* and *"desperately sick"*: *"The heart is deceitful above all things, and desperately sick; who can understand it?"* (ESV). The Bible also tells us, *"Guard your heart above all else, for it determines the course of your life"* (Proverbs 4:23 NLT; see also NIV). Another translation of this verse says that out of the heart springs forth every issue of life. (See KJV.) Think about that, friend: *every issue of life.* In other words, the condition of our hearts determines the quality and success of our lives and our relationships with others.

GOD'S REMEDIES FOR HURTING HEARTS

Let's take a moment to recognize that the Lord our God has the remedy for every one of the life issues and unhealed areas within our hearts and souls. God is clear about His desire to make us whole and put us on the right path to a great and satisfying life:

+ Psalm 147:3: "*He heals the brokenhearted and binds up their wounds*" (various translations).

+ Psalm 23:3: "*He restores my soul. He leads me in paths of righteousness for his name's sake*" (ESV).

+ Isaiah 41:10: "*Don't be afraid, for I am with you. Don't be discouraged, for I am your God. I will strengthen you and help you. I will hold you up with my victorious right hand*" (NLT).

+ John 10:10: "[Jesus said,] '*The thief's purpose is to steal and kill and destroy. My purpose is to give them a rich and satisfying life*'" (NLT).

+ 2 Timothy 1:7: "*For God has not given us a spirit of fear and timidity, but of power, love, and self-discipline* ['*a sound mind*' KJV, NKJV]" (NLT).

God has the remedy for it all!

We must truly come to understand that most relationship issues stem from wounded and unhealed hearts. Broken hearts lead to broken relationships. When the heart is injured through sin, stagnation, and/or painful experiences, it becomes defective. That defectiveness can take various forms. Wounded hearts produce emotional turmoil that bleeds into people's daily lives. An unhealed heart is selfish, unmotivated, desperate, bitter, and dangerous. It will compromise, betray, spew insults, embrace promiscuity, develop addictions, prompt violent action, and generally produce sadness and defeated living. A lack of participation and motivation in a relationship can sometimes be equally as damaging as destructive behaviors. All such responses are clear signs of wounded hearts and lives uninspired by Jesus.

Unfortunately, many people reject the truth that a personal, active relationship with Jesus is the foundational building block of all personal relationships, including marriage. When our hearts are healed and whole, we can love right and live right. We can walk in forgiveness. We can move forward in our lives no matter how deeply we've been hurt or have hurt others. A healed heart is no longer in bondage to the hurts of this world or the mundane routines of daily life. It becomes motivated to live and love again. Arguments rooted in bitterness disappear. Negative feelings toward ourselves dissipate. Hopelessness fades away as joy fills our hearts and lives. We are equipped to experience joyful, healthy, purposeful, and fulfilling relationships. We become capable of loving ourselves and others the way God intended.

FINDING PURE LOVE THROUGH A HEALED HEART

I wrote earlier that the heart's main spiritual and emotional purpose is to give and receive love, but the desire to love and the ability to love are two entirely different things. I shared this concept with regard to my relationship with Darryl. Now, let's view this same point through the lens of a different relationship. I deeply cared about my children but was incapable of fully loving them in the way God intended for me to love them. In other words, I felt incredible love for them and desired to love them as they deserved to be loved, but I lacked the character to live out that love. Let me say it again, friend: desire is not enough, in any relationship. We must become *capable* of loving.

Sincere love is the foundation of any healthy relationship, whether it is a parent-child relationship, a marriage, a dating relationship, or a friendship. As we have seen, unless we understand and practice genuine love, we can inflict great damage on ourselves and others. The good news is that our hearts can be healed so that we can love again—or perhaps really love for the first time in our lives. The following are crucial principles for understanding genuine love and finding pure love through a healed heart.

1. God is love. In my struggles to receive love, I was ignorant of what real love was. I was oblivious to God's definition of love because I didn't recognize that *God Himself is love*. First John 4:7–8 makes this truth plain: "*Dear friends, let us continue to love one another, for love comes from God.*

Anyone who loves is a child of God and knows God. But anyone who does not love does not know God, for God is love" (NLT). When we enter into a relationship with God, we experience His love, and that same love is born in our hearts through the Holy Spirit, enabling us to extend it to others. Many people are trying to love one another without having a strong, active, personal relationship with Jesus. That kind of love is based on self-will and human effort alone, which ultimately leads to selfishness and even sin. It causes division, stagnation, lack of motivation, dwindling desire for the other person, and many other harmful consequences. But when we have Christ as our foundation, His grace will cover us, the Holy Spirit's conviction will keep us, and genuine love will thrive within us.

2. We are only able to love because God first loved us. *"For God so loved the world, that he gave his only Son, that whoever believes in him should not perish but have eternal life"* (John 3:16 ESV). *"In this is love, not that we have loved God but that he loved us and sent his Son to be the propitiation for our sins. Beloved, if God so loved us, we also ought to love one another.... We love because he first loved us"* (1 John 4:10–11, 19 ESV). Again, God is the foundation of genuine love because we wouldn't know love without Him. It is He who first loved us—completely and unconditionally. And He continually reaches out to us with *compassion, forgiveness,* and *reconciliation,* all of which He commands us to practice and exchange within our relationships. Don't miss these three foundational relationship components, which are crucial for a relationship to thrive!

3. We understand the nature of God's love through His Word. The Bible, the manual God has given us for life, describes in great detail how genuine love is restored, experienced, and expressed after being damaged, betrayed, or broken. In this chapter, I have included some of those passages. The thirteenth chapter of 1 Corinthians is another wonderful passage on the nature of God's love. I encourage you to read and meditate on these passages until the words enter deeply into your heart and mind and begin to transform you.

4. Genuine love, the love God intended for us to exhibit, is evidenced not just in our feelings or verbal professions but through our actions. *"Little children, let us not love in word or talk but in deed and in truth"* (1 John 3:18 ESV). Real love is sacrificial. It gives rather than takes.

It backs up declarations of "I love you" with intentional actions, affection, and honest living. No secrets. No selfishness. No stagnation. *Love* is an action word.

There is a huge difference between love as the world defines it and love as the central aspect of God's nature. The world's view of love is distorted and destructive. It sells love as sex, pleasure, self-indulgence, and the means to meet your deepest wants and desires. It thinks that outward experiences such as romantic getaways and shared adventures can create and complete love. It tricks you into believing that another person will complete you. Wrong. Truth be told, it is your wholeness in God that makes you complete. The world frequently searches for outward solutions to remedy inward issues that can only be solved by forgiveness and restoration in God. Such counterfeit love will never be enough to satisfy our deepest longings. The result of this erroneous mindset is that love is the most misunderstood, misused, and improperly pursued entity in the world.

God's love is rooted and grounded in faith and Christlike character. It anchors itself deeply in commitment and faithfulness and is stronger than our feelings and emotions. When we receive God's pure love, we desire and seek to fulfill His purposes, not our selfish wants, within our relationships. Such love can only be manifested through the plan, design, and direction of God as we follow His Word and His ways.

I love how *The Message* Bible conveys the most popular biblical passage on love. These verses illustrate how love acts, walks, and talks. They describe how genuine love is expressed. As you read the following passage, think about this: what if both parties within a relationship intentionally loved one another in this manner?

> *Love never gives up. Love cares more for others than for self. Love doesn't want what it doesn't have. Love doesn't strut, doesn't have a swelled head, doesn't force itself on others, isn't always "me first," doesn't fly off the handle, doesn't keep score of the sins of others, doesn't revel when others grovel, takes pleasure in the flowering of truth, puts up with anything, trusts God always, always looks for the best, never looks back, but keeps going to the end.* (1 Corinthians 13:4–7 MSG)

If living according to this type of love seems like a mighty mountain to climb, that's because it is! Again, you can only love in this way by first receiving God's love. And if you've been hurt, you can only do this through His healing and transformative power, which comes exclusively through the Holy Spirit. God alone can heal. And healing is what this book is all about.

God gives us great hope regarding the issue of our damaged hearts. He makes it possible for us to be right with Him and with others by giving us a new heart and a new mind. This is God's amazing promise to us: *"I will give you a new heart, and I will put a new spirit in you. I will take out your stony, stubborn heart and give you a tender, responsive heart"* (Ezekiel 36:26 NLT). This new heart is made up of His character and nature.

I wrote earlier that we need to discover and establish a right standard of value and self-worth for ourselves in order to have healthy relationships. That standard is based on what I have described in this chapter: the love of God for us, the great value He places on us, the purposes He has for us. How does God begin this mighty, transformative work in our hearts? He starts with forgiveness. Our hearts are severely desperate, wicked, and wounded when they are separated from God and left in the "land of unforgiveness." Before healing can really begin, forgiveness must settle in. It's time to forgive, friend. It's time for a new heart.

COURAGE CHOICES FOR YOUR HEALING

1. How does the world define love? How does that definition differ from God's love? Write a brief description of the qualities of God's love as revealed in the Scriptures. What does it mean to you that God loves you in that way?

2. After reading the definition of codependency in this chapter, consider how you might be enabling another person in your life and losing yourself in the process. What steps can you follow to start taking back your life?

3. If you have struggled in your romantic relationships, ask yourself the following questions from the section "Answering the 'Why's'":

   a. Why did I choose these partners?

   b. Why did I allow them to pick me?

   c. When things started to go very wrong in the relationships, why did I stay?

   d. Why did I marry partners in the midst of their mess, their empty promises, and their inability to truly love me?

After honestly answering these questions, seek the counsel of a godly therapist or mature Christian leader or friend who can help you see yourself and the other parties in your various relationships as God sees you. You need support to heal from your tendency to fall into destructive relationships. Spend more time in God's Word, in prayer, and in fellowship with other believers as you allow God to continue the healing process in you.

4. What high standards of living and loving will you adopt and remain faithful to? Write them down and keep them where you can refer to them often. Is there any area of your life where you need to take a stand for godliness and let God have His way in a situation, rather than trying to handle it your way, to your detriment? If so, with the counsel and support of mature believers, take that step and commit the situation to the Lord.

5. From the section "Finding Pure Love Through a Healed Heart," what are the four principles for understanding genuine love and finding pure love?

4

FORGIVENESS:
A CRUCIAL STEP TO FREEDOM

The power of God is greater than our deepest wounds and hurts. His power gives us the ability to forgive ourselves and others for past wrongs, mistakes, betrayals, and dysfunctional living. Forgiveness is a crucial step of the journey that leads us to freedom.

In my life, I have had to extend and receive much forgiveness. I have committed a lot of wrongs, and many wrongs have been committed against me. Through experience, I have come to learn that God is always trying to make us well as quickly as possible, and one of the main ways He does this is through forgiveness. Out of His great love for us, He created the process of healing to restore what human beings damage, break, or harm through our sinful nature. Not one of us is perfect, and we all fall short of the glory of God. (See Romans 3:23.) Sometimes, the mistakes we make are little; other times, they are deeply damaging. God knows the depths of the wrongs we have done, as well as of the wrongs that have been perpetrated against us. But although we are imperfect people, we serve a perfect and powerful God. He makes restoration possible. He gives us new beginnings as gifts just waiting for us to receive with joy, like children opening their presents on Christmas morning. He is the Waymaker in every situation.

STRUGGLING TO FORGIVE

Over the years, countless people have shared with me how they sought the Lord to experience the power of forgiveness. They prayed, declared Scriptures over their lives, and made their confessions of forgiveness with confidence. They proclaimed what seemed like magical phrases—"God, forgive me; God, I forgive them"—but they got only as far into the healing process as their verbal confession.

Notice that I said *healing* process, not *forgiveness* process. Many people, including myself, have experienced a degree of relief through offering professions of forgiveness, but it didn't last. When this happened to me, I thought, "How can I be a Jesus-loving, Bible-obeying, God-fearing woman and still be very much bound to my past and my pain?" I finally realized that the bigger picture of freedom requires more steps than merely the confession of forgiveness.

Forgiveness is one step on the pathway of freedom within the healing journey. This journey includes practices like releasing vengeance over to the Lord, reexamining ourselves and our relationships, and establishing healthy boundaries. It also demands an understanding that rebuilding trust with those who have offended us and those whom we have offended can be painful and requires time to achieve.

The truth is that forgiveness is an instantaneous gift from God given to us at salvation as a divine exchange. And it is a spiritual power that continuously works within us throughout our lives. We freely receive forgiveness from God, and we can freely give it away to others through His grace. Forgiveness cannot be earned, worked on, or worked out. We did not accomplish forgiveness ourselves, and therefore it is not ours to withhold or reject from ourselves or others. Forgiveness comes through the complete and finished work of the cross of Jesus Christ alone.

When you put your trust in the Lord by obeying His Word and relying on the Holy Spirit, you will change. You will heal. You will become transformed. You will enter into a place of power and peace. Then, gradually, as you make one courageous choice at a time, what once held you hostage— the offenses, the regrets, the heartaches, the sufferings, and everything else that stems from the poison of unforgiveness—will loosen their grip on you until, eventually, they will have no power over you whatsoever.

Now, let's get to work!

LET THE HEALING BEGIN

I want to offer three big ideas with accompanying passages of Scripture that will challenge your wounded feelings, strengthen your faith, and set you up for experiencing freedom through the power of forgiveness.

1. FORGIVENESS IS NOT OPTIONAL...IF YOU WANT TO BE FREE

If you forgive those who sin against you, your heavenly Father will forgive you. But if you refuse to forgive others, your Father will not forgive your sins. (Matthew 6:14–15 NLT)

In this passage, Jesus teaches us that forgiving others is not optional if we want to be forgiven and free. Forgiveness is *the way* to freedom. It's God's method of cleansing our hearts so we can become healed and whole. Therefore, if you want to be forgiven, you must forgive. It's a command to follow if you want to leave the pain of the past behind.

When you've been hurt by someone, or when someone you love has been hurt by another person, you may hesitate to forgive the offender because you feel overwhelming disappointment, betrayal, rage, resentment, or bitterness. You may say things to God like, "But You don't know what they did to me" or "You don't know how badly they hurt my child/spouse/ friend. If You did, You wouldn't ask me to forgive them!" In the midst of their pain and anger, many people outright refuse to forgive. A common response I hear from people is, "I will never, *ever* forgive so-and-so!" I can empathize with these powerful emotional responses. Why would God ask us to forgive someone despite the terrible and wicked things they have done? It seems unfair! Why isn't there another option or way out?

Are you struggling to forgive someone? Do you have a family member or friend who is having a hard time forgiving? (Is someone having a hard time forgiving you?) Maybe you think, "But, Tracy, doesn't my hurt count for something?" Of course it does! And God wants to heal your hurt. But the only way to start the process is to forgive.

Jesus took all our sins and wounds to the cross. He also paid the price for every injustice, every violation, every harm, and every wrong that has ever been committed against us. He made the way for us to be healed and set free. Forgiveness is His way. Jesus's provision on the cross gives us the healing power that will make us whole. Jesus doesn't want to harm us. He wants to heal us!

Forgiving ourselves and others is not only the gateway to healing, but it is also the greatest expression of our faith in Jesus Christ. When we withhold forgiveness, we reject our faith in Christ, His finished work on the cross, *and* our healing. We deny Jesus access to do His mighty work of restoration in our lives through the Holy Spirit. The Holy Spirit is a gentleman and will not trespass on our free will. We cannot receive healing without first forgiving others or asking God to forgive us. Invite Jesus to do His mighty work in you so you can begin to live again, friend. Receive God's forgiveness, and then forgive others. Remember, if you have not yet put your faith in Jesus Christ and received God's forgiveness, you won't have access to the power of full forgiveness through Christ.

FORGIVENESS IS GOD'S METHOD OF CLEANSING OUR HEARTS SO WE CAN BECOME HEALED AND WHOLE.

2. FORGIVE NOW SO THAT A ROOT OF BITTERNESS WILL NOT GROW

Therefore, if you are presenting your offering at the altar, and there you remember that your brother has something against you, leave your offering there before the altar and go; first be reconciled to your brother, and then come and present your offering. (Matthew 5:23–24 NASB)

Jesus teaches us that forgiveness should not be delayed. We must do it quickly. You may be thinking, "This is good stuff, Tracy, but I'm not ready to forgive that person just yet. I'm still *working on* forgiving them. I promise, I'll forgive when I am ready!"

Do you feel convicted to forgive but are delaying your obedience because you are "working on" forgiveness? I have read many books that try to teach people how to work on accomplishing or achieving forgiveness. Let me empower you with this truth: it is impossible! The work of forgiveness was already accomplished in Jesus Christ through His finished work on the cross.

Have you ever heard a person say to someone who has hurt or betrayed them, "You broke my forgiveness"? No, because forgiveness doesn't work that way. As the complete work of Jesus Christ, forgiveness can never be broken, undone, or changed; therefore, it can never be worked on, accomplished, or achieved through human effort. What people say instead is, "You broke my heart!" or "You broke my trust!"

Here is an example of a truthful and empowering response when forgiveness is required and healing is needed: "I forgive you, but I do not trust you, and I need time to heal." You have forgiven immediately, and yet you have clearly stated the issue: it will require time for you to work on the process of healing so you can trust that person once again. If the person does not change the behavior that caused the harm or refuses to get help, you may need to establish boundaries within the healing process. I discuss building trust and establishing boundaries in the next two chapters of this book.

However, you are still very much empowered in the midst of your pain through Jesus's way of healing your heart, even if your loved one does not want to change. But this is how you regain your power for living while obeying Jesus's commands. He never leaves you in a position of hopelessness or helplessness. You are always empowered to safeguard your life and establish boundaries for your own well-being so that you have the ability to move forward.

To summarize, when your trust is broken, your heart becomes damaged, and it is necessary to do some repair work in order to experience healing. We start the journey of healing by taking the first step into it, which is forgiveness. When we forgive, we can begin the work of rebuilding trust. If you wait to forgive, you delay the healing process and your own journey to freedom! You risk developing a root of bitterness that will keep you bound to your hurt. God does not want bitterness to take root in your heart, threatening your ability to love and to be loved. "*See to it that no one falls short of the grace of God and that no bitter root grows up to cause trouble and defile* many" (Hebrews 12:15 NIV). Never again withhold or delay forgiveness. Forgive, and do so immediately! You're worth the freedom that awaits you.

3. FORGIVE—AND KEEP FORGIVING— TO KEEP YOUR HEART CLEANSED AND HEALTHY

Then Peter came to Jesus and asked, "Lord, how many times shall I forgive my brother or sister who sins against me? Up to seven times?" Jesus answered, "I tell you, not seven times, but seventy-seven times."
(Matthew 18:21–22 NIV)

Here, Jesus offers a spiritual principle that forgiveness is ongoing. It is not a onetime deal. In other words, we are to forgive others over and over again for either the same offense or new wrongs. Every day presents us with opportunities to become offended, even by those we love. For instance, you will have to forgive your spouse for various transgressions throughout your marriage, and you will even need to forgive yourself throughout your lifetime for wrongs you commit.

This command by Jesus to continually forgive can be confusing and even painful to obey. Does it mean we should tolerate sinful behavior, infidelity, betrayals, or abuse? Does it mean we should let someone walk all over us like a doormat? Absolutely not! Jesus is telling us to always forgive so that we may keep our own hearts cleansed and healthy. Again, forgiveness is the cleansing agent of the heart that sets it up for the healing process. But, as I mentioned earlier, we must also use wisdom and establish boundaries when the offender is stuck in a cycle of sin. We are Christians, not doormats. Forgive and then stand firm by refusing to tolerate repeated sinful behaviors, and be careful not to enable the other person in their dysfunctional lifestyle.

CLEARING UP MISCONCEPTIONS ABOUT FORGIVENESS

We may have misconceptions about forgiveness that make forgiving others even more difficult. Let's clear up some common misconceptions about forgiveness and establish some truths in their place.

FORGIVENESS DOES NOT EXCUSE OR CONDONE WHAT HAPPENED TO YOU

When you forgive someone, it does not mean you are saying what the person did is okay. I believe we absorb this kind of thinking early in childhood. Picture a playdate with two toddlers. One child does something mean or inappropriate to the other child, such as take away his toy. Horrified, the parent of the child who took away the toy makes him tell his friend, "I'm sorry." The parent of the wronged child makes her say to the child who was just forced to apologize, "It's okay." And that's the end of that.

The thing is, it's not "okay." The child may not have taken the toy out of meanness, but he still needs to learn to share and respect other people's belongings. Over the years, I have come to discover that many people have never learned how to seek and give actual forgiveness. God is very clear in His Word that it's never okay for us to be harmed by anyone or to harm someone else. And when a wrong is committed, forgiveness and healing are needed.

I believe we need to be taught, as children and adults, to ask for forgiveness instead of merely saying "I'm sorry." Genuine forgiveness has great power. When we seek forgiveness with sincere hearts, it produces godly sorrow within us, turning us away from wrong behaviors and repetitive offenses. Our hearts are drawn to God in repentance, and we seek reconciliation with Him and other people. Second Corinthians 7:10 says, *"For the kind of sorrow God wants us to experience leads us away from sin and results in salvation. There's no regret for that kind of sorrow. But worldly sorrow, which lacks repentance* [turning away from sin], *results in spiritual death"* (NLT). Powerful words!

When we see our sins, our offenses, and our wrongs through God's eyes, the Holy Spirit produces a deep sorrow and sense of conviction in our hearts. This changes us in such a way that the wrong things we have done begin to sicken us, and we never want to hurt anyone in the same ways again. Then, when we humble ourselves before the Lord and confess our sins to Him, He changes our hearts. We turn toward Him and away from the sinful words and actions that harm ourselves and others. This is true repentance.

Saying "I'm sorry" does not possess the same power. Many times, it merely means that we regret we got caught or that we feel bad temporarily. Such reactions are not transformative enough to change our wrong behavior or create an awareness of how our actions have affected or hurt other people. This reality is evident when someone says to you, "I'm sorry," but then, perhaps a day, a week, or a month later, they do the same thing they said they were sorry for. That person has not experienced a genuine change of heart from God. I call this behavior being stuck in a cycle of sin, a cycle of repetitive bad behaviors and betrayal. The individual's character is still deficient, and their old wounds remain unhealed.

So, again, let me emphasize that when someone hurts us deeply, it is wrong and unacceptable. God knows it is wrong. And, likely, the person will experience consequences for those destructive actions. I spent many years dealing with the consequences of living my life separated from Christ. I still deal with some of those consequences. Specific ones will likely stay with me throughout my lifetime. But let me encourage you: there is grace for our lifelong consequences as well. Today, the Spirit of God and His healing power are alive inside of me. The sins and wounds of my past life are dead. Yes, I remember them, but they no longer have power over me. They don't own me, my relationships, or my destiny. I no longer act out or check out because of them. Nor do they hinder my relationships, my present, or my future. I am no longer the person I used to be. I am a new creation in Christ Jesus with a new heart and life. I am completely forgiven, and so are you, friend, if you belong to Christ Jesus.

Forgiveness is not a feeling. Instead, as I previously emphasized, to forgive is an act of faith that follows the commands of Scripture. Jesus tells us to forgive. He does not condone the wrongs committed against us, but, through forgiveness, He leads us into freedom. Don't delay forgiving others. Remember, forgiveness is God's cleansing agent for the heart in preparation for His healing power that makes you new.

JESUS TELLS US TO FORGIVE. HE DOES NOT CONDONE THE WRONGS COMMITTED AGAINST US, BUT, THROUGH FORGIVENESS AND THE HEALING PROCESS, HE LEADS US INTO FREEDOM.

FORGIVENESS DOES NOT LEAVE ROOM FOR PERSONAL VENGEANCE

In a previous chapter, I alluded to how, at the age of eight, I was repeatedly molested by an older man in our neighborhood, and I also experienced rape as an adult through my substance-abuse lifestyle and careless living. I put myself in harm's way day after day and year after year. Yet, regardless of the danger to which I exposed myself, I did not deserve the evil that was inflicted upon me. Victims of abuse should never carry the guilt of their abusers.

I struggled with anger over what my attackers had perpetrated against me. I wanted them to pay for their vile crimes. I wanted them to hurt as badly as I had been hurt. And I wanted vengeance against them. I wanted my pain and hate to mean something. The dictionary defines *vengeance* as "infliction of injury, harm, humiliation, or the like, on a person by another who has been harmed by that person; violent revenge" and "an act or opportunity of inflicting such trouble."[4] Just as I did, those who desire vengeance, or who actually pursue it, want the person who hurt either them or their loved one to suffer just as much as they have suffered—or even more so.

Over time, as I grew in Christ, I learned that vengeance isn't mine to pursue or dole out. And I discovered that the hate within my heart would never serve me well. Instead, it would only destroy me. I learned to view vengeance from God's standpoint. The Lord tells us to forgive and let Him handle the distressing situation: "*Vengeance is Mine, and recompense; their foot shall slip in due time; for the day of their calamity is at hand, and the things to come hasten upon them*" (Deuteronomy 32:35 NKJV). I especially like how the *New Living Translation* renders this verse: "*I will take revenge; I will pay them back. In due time their feet will slip. Their day of disaster will arrive, and their destiny will overtake them.*" And Romans 12:19 tells us, "*Dear friends, never take revenge. Leave that to the righteous anger of God. For the Scriptures say, 'I will take revenge; I will pay them back', says the LORD*" (NLT).

God wants you to move as far away from the offense as possible. He wants you focused on healing and getting beyond the all-consuming pain that robs you of peace and joy. God did just that for me by healing me of the pain of the sexual abuse I experienced. He also saved my marriage when the emotional effects of the abuse constructed a barrier between my husband and me.

---

4. *Dictionary.com*, s.v. "vengeance," https://www.dictionary.com/browse/vengeance.

Although, as I described in the previous chapter, Darryl had received Jesus Christ as Savior and was following the Lord, after we first got married, he reopened the door to some old friends and fell back into his old ways for a few years. I will talk more about this in a later chapter. But after Darryl became right with God through his own healing journey, I became the apple of his eye. He is one of the most powerful men of God I know. He loves me and our children unconditionally and with a passion and power that no evil can penetrate. Over time, my husband would become a prayer warrior through his daily study of the Bible and spiritual mentorship with strong men of God. I didn't realize how much I would need him and his power in the Lord until one particular night when my past caught up with me.

I had thought that if I truly fell in love, got married, and lived right, the tormenting memories and the fear, anger, and pain from the violent sexual assault I had endured a few years before my marriage to Darryl would just go away. I couldn't have been more wrong. I did fall deeply in love with Darryl, and I was fully committed to Christ. But after Darryl and I married, I longed for a magical transformation to take place that would allow me to love my husband with a free and open heart. For years, I waited for this to occur until the Holy Spirit convicted my heart to make a change.

Prior to that time, even though I was a Christian, I did not follow all of God's commands. Specifically, I had never forgiven my rapists; therefore, I could not enter into the process of healing that you are learning about in this book. I had never dealt with this issue with God, myself, or Darryl. I never talked about it, not even to the Lord. It was too painful, too dark, and too overwhelming to even think about, let alone process emotionally and spiritually. But my heart issues were negatively affecting my life and my marriage. Whether I wanted to address them or not, these unresolved emotions were casting a long, dark shadow on my attempts to move forward in life.

When Darryl firmly committed his life to Christ, he became the light that shined in this very dark place within me. Although he didn't know the details of the assault, he knew something was wrong with me. My issue was affecting our physical relationship. Because of the sexual assault I had endured, it was extremely difficult for me to be intimate with Darryl in the marriage bed. His simply touching me made me visibly uncomfortable. At times, every touch was a reminder of the attack. I would fight emotionally and mentally just to get through our private times together. A husband knows where there is a great disconnect with his wife. Because of how I responded when we were intimate, Darryl would feel guilty every time he touched me. He just didn't know why. It was not intentional, but I was making him pay for the wounds of my past.

Darryl did not know that I was full of rage. As I said, I wanted my attackers to pay for what they had done. I wished evil on them. I wanted them to suffer. These wicked men had destroyed my sense of safety and shattered my soul. I was also angry at God, blaming Him for not rescuing me. I felt weak, ashamed, unlovable, dirty, and hopeless. I also felt like a victim, and I hated that feeling. These emotions and thoughts stuck with me over the years. They changed my personality. Before the attack, I had been fun and outgoing. After the attack, I became more withdrawn, angry, short-tempered, and emotionally distant, even with my husband. One night, Darryl couldn't take it anymore. Seeing the pain in my eyes broke his heart. He demanded, in love, that I share the details of what had happened to me so we could overcome this obstacle, and I could heal. He wanted me to be well and for our marriage to be whole.

Finally, I opened up to Darryl and told him about the violent attack. He listened carefully, and then he immediately took a firm stand as the head of our marriage and told me we were going to pray together. We got out of bed and knelt down. He held my hands and began to pray in such a powerful way. He called down the heavens and asked God to heal my heart. He also asked God to show him how to help me become well. His prayer was lengthy, and as he continued, every word was more powerful than the last. We ended this precious time together full of tears and in each other's arms. As I cried, he just held me and told me it was going to be okay.

A few days later, we sat down and talked at length about a solution. He asked me what he could do to help me get through my pain. I gave him a list of what not to say and what never to ask of me in the marriage bed. We also discussed my triggers and how we could work through them together. Finally, he committed to pray over me and over us through this season.

As Darryl and I prayed together regularly, the Lord started leading me to also seek Him personally, just God and me. The closer I drew to God, the more I could sense Him guiding me to forgive my attackers. Forgiveness, in the process of healing I have been emphasizing, was the first step to my receiving healing for this deeply painful wound. Remember, forgiveness is the gateway to healing! After years of harboring unforgiveness and delaying my healing, I finally submitted to these words of Jesus: *"If you forgive those who sin against you, your heavenly Father will forgive you. But if you refuse to forgive others, your Father will not forgive your sins"* (Matthew 6:14–15 NLT).

It was time for me to forgive so I could become healed, free, and whole again. I set aside a quiet time one morning to do this, making sure I was not on a time limit. I hit my knees and asked God to hear and receive my every word. Not one part of me "felt" like forgiving my attackers. But I desperately needed to be free. I wanted my heart and my life back. I wanted to love without limits. I wanted to walk in the freedom God calls each of us to. So, I wrote a letter to God in my journal. Then, I spoke the words out loud: "I forgive those who attacked me, Lord! I release them into Your hands—everything they did and said to me, as well as every bit of hate, anger, rage, and pain that is consuming me!" I not only allowed God into this unhealed area of my life, but I also released my attackers into His hands and myself into His heart. I finally forgave!

As the words left my mouth, I couldn't stop weeping. The tears flowed for hours. At the same time, I felt the peace of God literally come over me. I knew He was embracing me and covering me with His love. I also knew my obedience to Jesus Christ did not condone what my rapists had done. I started studying Scriptures about vengeance like the ones we looked at earlier, as well as this one from 2 Thessalonians:

> *God is just: He will pay back trouble to those who trouble you and give relief to you who are troubled, and to us as well. This will happen when the Lord Jesus is revealed from heaven in blazing fire with his powerful angels.* (2 Thessalonians 1:6–7 NIV)

I finally accepted the reality that vengeance belongs to God, not to me. And God's promise in 2 Thessalonians 1:6–7 came true for me. The Lord removed my troubled heart and brought me relief: He gave me peace, the tangible evidence of His healing power. With the psalmist, I declared,

"Fret not yourself because of evildoers; be not envious of wrongdoers! For they will soon fade like the grass and wither like the green herb" (Psalm 37:1–2 ESV).

Darryl and I chose to receive healing God's way. When I shared my secret with my husband and brought the darkness into the light, Darryl brought my need before the Lord, where it belonged, and the power of God started to fill both of our hearts. Then, I finally faced what had happened to me by forgiving my attackers, placing myself in God's hands, and trusting Him with the rage and thoughts of vengeance I had so deeply harbored. Over time, the Holy Spirit revealed to me the safeguards I needed within our marriage bed. He helped me find a way to feel protected and enjoy being intimate with my husband. When I chose faith over my feelings and became obedient to God's Word, the barrier of unforgiveness was torn down, and the healing power of God became fully alive inside of me. I intentionally released the past by focusing on my spiritual growth and investing my time in productive endeavors that resulted in great success and personal advancements in my life.

After I forgave my attackers and started receiving the truth of God's Word, I felt I had come full circle. Today, Darryl and I are healed on the inside and are free to love one another without the pain of our pasts stealing the richness of our present! We have used the same process for other difficulties within our marriage that needed healing, such as adulteries, addictions, bankruptcy, and all the other ways we harmed and betrayed ourselves and each other. Now, I am well, he is well, and our marriage is whole because we have chosen to forgive and to live life God's way.

My friend, rather than withholding forgiveness, and instead of fantasizing about hurting, or seeking to hurt, those who have hurt you, surrender those feelings and thoughts to God. He can handle them. Focus on reinventing yourself and beginning again. Dare to dream once more, and move in that direction. Peace, joy and happiness reside there.

I INTENTIONALLY RELEASED THE PAST BY FOCUSING ON MY SPIRITUAL GROWTH AND INVESTING MY TIME IN PRODUCTIVE ENDEAVORS THAT RESULTED IN GREAT SUCCESS AND PERSONAL ADVANCEMENTS IN MY LIFE.

FORGIVENESS DOES NOT ALWAYS MEAN RECONCILIATION

Just because you forgive someone doesn't mean you also allow them the right to be in your life. In some cases, relationships will have to end. This is true of an abusive or toxic relationship. Other situations may involve reconciliation but will require strong boundaries. There are different levels of trust and commitment within relationships that require definition and specific direction. To determine this definition and receive direction, you should pray, read the Bible, and seek wise counsel. Then you will know if and when to sever ties with anyone. Again, if you are married, you are in covenantal relationship and should seek godly counsel regarding these steps. As I mentioned previously, Darryl and I have written a book entitled *The Imperfect Marriage: Help for Those Who Think It's Over*, which deals with difficult marital issues and how to seek reconciliation. You may be experiencing the residual effects of someone's stony, stubborn, and cold heart, but you are not helpless. You can forgive and take a stand in love, determining what boundaries need to be enforced.

FORGIVENESS DOES NOT MEAN A BROKEN RELATIONSHIP WILL BE MAGICALLY REPAIRED AS IF NOTHING EVER HAPPENED

Have you ever been betrayed by someone and forgiven them but wonder why you just can't forget what happened and move on? If so, remember that forgiveness, healing, rebuilding trust, and setting healthy boundaries are all active components of your journey to freedom. As I noted previously, you may forgive someone but still not trust them. The journey is not over when you say, "I forgive you." It has only just begun. Further work needs to be done. Healing and rebuilding trust need to take place, and both of those aspects take time.

In chapter 1, I described how I chose to sign over custody of my children to my ex-husband. That was the most painful decision I have ever had to make. For years, my relationship with my sons was strained; at times, it was nonexistent. The emotional pain I experienced over this estrangement was unbearable. After years of my pleading with God for healing, and seeking His way of reconciliation through the Holy Spirit, He gave me the revelations of freedom I share in this book. I followed those revelations, and I am excited to tell you that I am now reconciled with my children.

Our relationships continue to become stronger and stronger every day. However, I didn't get to that place overnight. It didn't happen without much struggle, tension, and tears—on both their part and mine.

After I finally came to the place of experiencing God's forgiveness within my own heart, I started praying for the courage to ask my children for their forgiveness. When they were young, there was not much I could legally do to visit or even speak with them very often. So, I learned to start praying for them and believing for reconciliation. I studied the Bible and other Christian materials to learn how to pray with power. I learned how to be filled with faith through God's Word. I learned what it meant to believe in what God could do, even when circumstances seemed impossible. (See, for example, Mark 10:27.)

As the boys grew older, I had more opportunities to see them, even though they were still living with their father. They started to recognize the woman of God I had become instead of the woman I used to be. They were now old enough to form their own opinions of me, new opinions based on the truth of what they were witnessing, not on what they knew from the past or what they had been told.

Here is a crucial point I do not want you to miss: had I not turned my life over to Jesus Christ and practiced every principle I share in this book, I would not be reconciled with my sons today! Had I made the choice to relapse, quit, or check out when times were tough and things did not go my way, I would not have the boys in my life right now. My life would not be powerful—full of purpose, family, and love—if I had chosen to turn back! If I had not truly surrendered to Jesus, participated in the process of change, lived out my new way of life, and walked in persevering faith, I might not even be here. If I had not engaged in consistent prayer, studied the Word of God, and allowed the Holy Spirit to abide in me, I would not be the changed woman that my sons could love and ultimately trust. Only Jesus can do this kind of transformative work. If you are in a situation similar to what I faced, know that if you go deep with Jesus *and* stay your course, you will get there. You will have a life filled with victories, joy, purpose, power, and peace!

One by one, and over a period of time, I approached each of my children separately and asked them to forgive me for all the wrongs I had committed against them and the hurt I had caused them. Each one reacted differently to my request. My oldest distanced himself from me off and on for years. He quickly forgave me, but he did not trust me—and rightfully so. Trust must be proven over time. That is how it is regained and rebuilt. At times, each of my sons expressed anger. Other times, we cried together. I had to give my boys a safe place to heal and not rush the process of reconciliation.

I also had to hear them express the wounds that were in their hearts. Just because I asked them for forgiveness did not mean they were okay. Even though my children forgave me, much healing had to take place within them and between us. Boundaries needed to be set in place. The kids asked a lot of questions. The big one was, "How do we know you will not relapse or leave us again?" I did not rush in with a blanket answer full of promises. The Holy Spirit gave me such wisdom at the time. I told them I believed we all needed to heal and that it would take time to rebuild trust between us. They agreed. I also told them they had to see a change in me through my actions and behaviors. They agreed to this, as well, and told me they appreciated hearing that truth.

Then, I asked each of my boys what they needed from me. They said things like allowing more time and space for them to process the situation, spending time together doing fun things and building new memories, talking together more, and seeing me exhibit consistent and healthy habits, behaviors, and actions. We made this agreement, and we have been on this journey ever since. For each of my children, healing was a process, and it came at different times and in different ways. I had to trust the Holy Spirit and be patient with them as they healed. I had to allow them their time, space, and individual ways of processing their healing.

Rebuilding these precious relationships took a long time, but things got better every year. There is progress amid the pain, and mini-victories within the battles. Each passing year brought more closeness, more joy, and more laughter. While I now have a close relationship with each of my sons, we are still working through some issues, and I believe we will overcome those as well.

TRUST GOD ON THE JOURNEY

Trusting God is essential in this journey of healing—in any journey, for that matter. God can only work at the level of willingness and obedience that we give Him. I believe that trusting Him is the ultimate test of faith. Again, forgiveness is not a feeling but rather faith in action through the power of the Holy Spirit. I don't know where I would be if I didn't trust God. Not in the amazing place of restoration I now enjoy, I can tell you that. I certainly wouldn't be living a restored life. Here is a greater thought: neither would my children. What a tragedy it would still be for them if I hadn't surrendered to Jesus, stayed on the right course, and entered into God's great forgiveness and healing power.

I encourage you to forgive yourself and others today. Trust God with all your heart. Trust Him in the process of your healing. Then watch as great things unfold!

If you have not yet accepted Jesus Christ as Your Savior and Lord, receiving His forgiveness, I want to provide an opportunity for you to give Jesus permission to come into your life and begin His mighty work of forgiveness within you. You can do so right now by praying this simple prayer. If you can, read the prayer out loud, and then let's continue on. You're worth it!

Dear Jesus, I open up my heart to You—a heart that needs healing, cleansing, and guidance. I ask You to forgive me for every sin and wrong I've ever committed. I surrender my guilt, pain, shame, regrets, and anger over to You. I believe that You died on the cross for every sin, and You were raised to life so that I may have a new life here on earth and eternal life with You in heaven. Come into my heart, Jesus, and take control of my life. I want to trust You as my Savior, my Healer, my Everything, and follow You from this day forward. In Your name, Jesus, I pray, amen.

COURAGE CHOICES FOR YOUR HEALING:

1. From the section "Let the Healing Begin," list the "three big ideas," their corresponding Scriptures, and the major points of revelation about forgiveness that stood out to you.

2. From the section "Clearing Up Misconceptions About Forgiveness," what are four misconceptions people often have about the nature of forgiveness?

3. One of the misconceptions about forgiveness is that it still leaves room for vengeance for wrongs committed against us. Consider the following questions:

    a. What is the definition of vengeance?

    b. What does the Bible say about vengeance?

    c. Will you release any thoughts of vengeance over to the Lord? Do so immediately, in your own words. It is a power choice within the healing process.

4. Why does God want us to forgive—immediately and repetitively?

5. Whom do you need to forgive?

    a. Make a list of everyone you need to forgive. Make sure your own name makes the list.

    b. Set aside a time when you can be alone and uninterrupted to pray the following prayer. Arrange to have someone available whom you can call if you need spiritual and emotional support after this process. Forgiving is freeing, yet it can also be a very emotional experience.

    c. As you pray, speak aloud the names of the people, including yourself, whom you are forgiving. Release them and yourself into the hands of almighty God.

Father, in the name of Jesus, I forgive _____ _____. I release them and every detail of the situation over to You, so that it will no longer have power over me, in Jesus's name. I release my entire being into Your hands. I will not harbor thoughts of punishment, vengeance, or self-harm. I enter into Your way of healing and restoration. I ask You to heal every part of me, including my heart, mind, emotions, body, and spirit. O God, heal even my memories so they will no longer have power over me. I trust that You are healing my wounds right now and setting me free. I abandon myself to You in full surrender. Have Your way in every part of my life. In the name of Jesus, amen and amen.

5

REBUILDING TRUST

When forgiveness is required, especially for a significant offense, it means that trust has been broken and needs to be rebuilt. Yet, as we have seen, before trust can be restored, God's supernatural work must clear the wreckage of sin's devastating impact. To experience spiritual and emotional healing, we must allow God to forgive us and enable us to forgive others through Jesus Christ's finished work on the cross.

Forgiveness, we have learned, is not optional. We forgive in obedience to Jesus's commands, and this allows our healing to begin. The mighty work of the Holy Spirit springs forth as we obey the principles of God's Word. This is God's way of healing and restoration. Remember, forgiveness is not the struggle. The struggle is our journey to healing from the pain of the betrayal. This struggle often involves the process of mending the trust that was broken; it requires a repentant heart and a demonstration of real change on the part of the offender, which takes time. While we have no authority to deem who is or isn't worthy of forgiveness, when it comes to rebuilding and bestowing trust, we absolutely can dictate the terms according to God's Word.

THE FOUNDATION OF ALL RELATIONSHIPS

God calls Christians to be trustworthy—men and women of integrity and honor. He wants us to be faithful, dependable, and safe with regard to others. Trust is the foundational building block of all positive relationships. If either party compromises or breaks trust, the relationship suffers, and the participants experience pain or loss—or both.

When we have been betrayed in some way, we often say things like the following to the one who has hurt us:

- "I can't rely on you."
- "I can't trust you to [fill in the blank]."
- "I don't believe you'll do the right thing."
- "I can't be intimate with you again until I'm ready."

Once we have forgiven our spouse, child, friend, in-law, or anyone else for an offense, then, and only then, can we embark on a journey of rebuilding trust. This process is often difficult because the effects of broken trust—pain, sorrow, frustration, anger, rage, resentment, and heartache—can lie dormant in our hearts like oxygen-starved embers. Broken trust leads to wounded hearts, hence the absolute need for healing to take place at the same time trust is being rebuilt.

WHAT IS TRUST?

I like to define trust as "the result of consistent behavior and dependability displayed over time." If you think about it, nearly every decision we make comes down to trusting in a particular outcome or result. For example, each one of our financial decisions comes with expectations or a level of trust that the outcome will be worth the money spent, the money saved, or the investment made. Or, when we purchase a product—anything from a blender to a high-priced automobile—we trust that the item we bought will do what it was designed and created to do. Most of us expect the same type of outcome in our relationships: we trust that people will live and act in the way in which God created us to live and act.

Actual trust—not just assumed trust—in a product or a person is established when that product or person does the right thing over and over again, displaying consistency. This is why it takes time to build trust and especially to rebuild it after it has been broken. The process doesn't happen overnight, and it doesn't automatically manifest simply because forgiveness has been extended to the offender.

When you are rebuilding trust within a broken relationship, it's important to remember the following principles, the first of which we just established:

- Trust is built over time. Time reveals the true character of a person.

- Different relationships involve different levels of trust. For example, a relationship with a spouse will require a deeper level of trust than a relationship with a distant relative.

- A person's character determines whether or not they are capable of loving themselves and others. An untrustworthy person is incapable of sustaining a healthy relationship with another person.

- Regaining trust requires more than just promising to act differently; it necessitates a demonstrable change in one's behavior. Such change can come only by a renovation of one's character through the power of God and the process of change. This process leads to transformation that lasts—a true renewal of the heart. Without this renewal, a person will remain stuck in a cycle of dysfunction and defeat.

Are you the one who is stuck in such a cycle, friend? Or is it a loved one? Is it both of you? Regardless, decide to take action today to start walking on the pathway to healing and transformation. Trust God and His process of change, even if your loved one chooses not to do so.

> **TRUST IS BUILT OVER TIME. TIME REVEALS THE TRUE CHARACTER OF A PERSON.**

DIFFERENCES BETWEEN FORGIVENESS AND TRUST

Ironically, people are quick to trust and slow to forgive. Yet this is the exact opposite of how God tells us to be. We are to forgive quickly, and then we can rebuild trust over time. In the previous chapter, we discussed some key biblical passages about forgiveness. The Bible also offers us much direction and guidance about trust. For example, remember what Proverbs 4:23 says: *"Guard your heart above all else, for it determines the course of your life"* (NLT). And Proverbs 25:19 warns, *"Trusting an unreliable person in a difficult time is like a rotten tooth or a faltering foot"* (HCSB).

Because forgiveness and trust are distinct, they need to be approached differently. Having covered the topic of forgiveness in the previous chapter, I now want to highlight the differences between forgiveness and trust. Some of the following areas may overlap, but this overview will help you begin to understand the concept of rebuilding trust with another person, or even with yourself.

FORGIVENESS	TRUST
Forgiveness is instant; it is an immediate step of obedience made in faith that opens the gateway to healing. It is the greatest expression of our faith and grants God full permission to enter into our hearts, allowing the supernatural healing power of the Holy Spirit to be activated instantly. To refuse to forgive is to deny our faith in Jesus and to reject every benefit accessible to us through His finished work on the cross. One of those benefits is healing. Don't delay, friend. Forgive and let healing have its way in you.	Trust and healing are a process. When trust has been violated, it takes time for the heart to heal and for trust to be rebuilt. Healing is not instant, and trust cannot be immediately restored. Many times, rebuilding trust will require us to guard our hearts with boundaries as the healing process takes place. Boundaries establish safe, clear terms for how we are going to proceed in our daily life in various situations. Implementing these terms requires a timely, intentional process, with God at the center of it all.

FORGIVENESS	TRUST
Forgiveness is a free gift we receive upon receiving salvation through Jesus Christ. Jesus demonstrated and accomplished forgiveness by His love, character, and finished work on the cross. Not one of us can prove to Jesus that we are worthy of forgiveness. None of us *is* worthy. Forgiveness is freely and instantly received by faith, and therefore it is also to be freely and immediately given by faith.	Trustworthiness is not a free gift. It is proven, earned, and accomplished over time. It is demonstrated by a person's consistent integrity, good character, reliability, and right actions. These are all evidence of a life transformed through repentance, expressed through a genuine commitment to Christ.
Forgiveness is never broken and therefore never needs to be "worked on" or accomplished. It is the finished work that Jesus Christ alone accomplished on the cross. It is not our work to do or a quest we can achieve. It is already completed. Done. Finished!	When we experience a betrayal or an offense, both our heart and trust become "broken." A mighty work is needed to accomplish restoration and freedom. The Holy Spirit is the Healer of hearts and will guide us in the step-by-step process of rebuilding trust over time as our healing takes place.
Forgiveness is not optional, and we do not get to choose whom we forgive. Forgiveness is a spiritual command that we must obey if we desire to be healed, whole, and free.	Trust is optional. We choose who to trust, and we must choose wisely. In any relationship, we need to allow time for the character of the other party to be revealed.

FORGIVENESS	TRUST
Forgiveness is always unmerited. No one has to prove to us they are worthy of forgiveness. None of us is worthy. God wants us to forgive all people freely so we can become free.	Trust must be earned. Proving trustworthiness is the responsibility of the one who violated the trust.
There are no "degrees" of forgiveness. It is all or nothing.	There are different degrees or levels of trust in relationships, depending on the nature of the relationships.
Forgiveness is God's operational system of cleansing and purifying the heart so healing can begin after offenses, injuries, and betrayals take place.	Trust is the foundation of all relationships. Relationships are built on trust and decimated when trust is broken. But, through the power of the Holy Spirit and the parties' obedience to God's way, trust can be rebuilt as a firm foundation once again.
Forgiveness is not to be our battle or struggle, nor withheld because of distressing emotions. Although it can feel painful to forgive, forgiveness is the most powerful step leading to healing and freedom. Jesus's sacrifice on the cross is the basis of all forgiveness and is the entryway to our ultimate freedom. His death brings us life, and life more abundantly, if we will receive that life by doing things God's way.	Healing is a painful battle, and rebuilding broken trust is a struggle. Trust is an exercise of mutual faithfulness among two or more parties. It becomes a battle, struggle, or issue when someone in the relationship commits a betrayal or offense that harms the parties and their relationships. A firm commitment to Christ, by obeying God's Word and ways, facilitates the process of healing and restoration after trust is broken.

TRUST FOLLOWS TRUE CHANGE

Genuine positive change in a person's life through the power of God breaks the cycle of sin that has kept that person untrustworthy and unreliable. Their transformation enables them to begin rebuilding the faith they have broken with their loved ones and friends. When seeking to reestablish trust with someone who has repeatedly hurt or betrayed you, look for real change and be careful not to be fooled by empty promises such as these:

+ "I've really changed."

+ "I'll start going to church with you."

+ "I won't squander our money."

+ "I'll get a steady job."

+ "I won't hurt you again."

These promises sound good, and people may be sincere when they speak them, but, in themselves, promises are not enough to rebuild trust. You need to realize that someone can make you promise after promise about how they have changed, and they can tell you everything they are going to do differently from now on. But, truth be told, until they have a genuine encounter with the Lord Jesus Christ, experience a heart transformation, commit their life to God, stay the course of restoration, and actively cultivate good character, their old habits will eventually resurface. They will be incapable of acting differently because they will still be the same person inside. They may have a desire to change, but their character defects will be ever present.

This is why trust cannot be rebuilt until the cycle of sin is broken. When someone is stuck in such a cycle, they are entrenched in dysfunction, exhibiting an unhealthy, toxic, and painful pattern of sinful behavior. They are rejecting Christ and the power of the Holy Spirit that can make them well and set them free. They continually say they are sorry, but they do not alter their attitudes or behaviors. Unless they truly repent—turn away from their sin and bad habits—they will not take the necessary action steps to change, and it's highly likely they will hurt you again. Once more, the real evidence is not what someone says but how that person acts and responds. The old adage "Actions speak louder than words" is really true. If you understand this reality, I promise that you will save yourself a lot of heartache and pain.

"Regret" is not the same thing as repentance. You can forgive your spouse, another family member, or a friend a thousand times, but until that person ends the extramarital affair, stops the lying, gets help for the addiction, or participates in the relationship properly, the process of rebuilding trust cannot begin.

I used to offer empty promises in all my relationships—with my kids, parents, ex-husbands, and friends. The relationships were different, but the way I related to people was the same. When I finally surrendered to God, I became a new creation and started living according to His ways, studying His Word, and taking responsibility for the things I needed to change in my life. When I confessed my sins to God and began obeying what He says, I experienced a change of heart that transformed my entire life and, in time, enabled me to rebuild the trust I had broken.

THE PROCESS OF REBUILDING TRUST

The following keys will guide you in the process of rebuilding trust in a broken relationship. Note that these suggestions apply to relationships where both parties are pursuing reconciliation. Not every relationship can be reconciled, and not all trust can be rebuilt to the same degree it was built prior to the offense. Be sure to evaluate your relationships and ask God to show you the correct course to take. As I mentioned previously, we will talk more about setting appropriate boundaries in the next chapter.

KEY #1: SUBMIT YOURSELF AND YOUR RELATIONSHIP TO GOD IN PRAYER

Proverbs 3:5–6 says, "*Trust in the* Lord *with all your heart; do not depend on your own understanding. Seek his will in all you do, and he will show you which path to take*" (NLT). We receive great power and clear direction when we pray. Submit your life to God and let Him guide you in handling a broken relationship the right way. Remember, you are not the savior of the relationship, of yourself, or of the other person involved—Jesus is. You can't fix the other person, but God can. Caution yourself not to be an enabler in the individual's cycle of sin. Listen carefully to the direction of the Holy Spirit as you pray and study God's Word. The right way to take will well up in your heart; when it does, obey the guidance you receive.

KEY #2: PRAY TOGETHER

If you are able to do so, pray with the person with whom you are seeking to rebuild trust. Every relationship is stronger when you pray together and ask for God's will to be done. This is because Jesus is present with you. Jesus said, *"For where two or three gather together as my followers, I am there among them"* (Matthew 18:20 NLT). Relationships that are united in prayer can endure many trials. Think of the marriage relationship as a triangle, with God at the top and the husband and wife positioned at opposite corners of the base. As the man and woman move closer to God in prayer, they simultaneously move closer to one another, and God's healing power becomes active. When God is at the center of our lives, the same process holds true for a parent-child relationship or a God-ordained friendship. In all relationships, praying together will accelerate the healing process.

RELATIONSHIPS THAT ARE UNITED IN PRAYER CAN ENDURE MANY TRIALS.

KEY #3: CREATE NEW MEMORIES

Creating new memories is healthy for any relationship, but it can be especially beneficial during the process of reestablishing trust. When trust has been violated, it is often hard to rebuild unity and closeness because old, painful memories keep resurfacing. Making new memories will help to replace ugly reminders of the past with hope and possibilities. You can create new memories together by engaging in a fun activity or visiting a place you've never been before, and taking pictures. This will give you the opportunity to celebrate new, shared experiences instead of rehashing the old hurts.

KEY #4: BE MINDFUL OF WHOSE ADVICE YOU TAKE

Who is giving you advice for your broken relationship? Is the guidance healthy and biblical? Beware of just blurting out your hurts and problems to anyone who will listen. Safeguarding your heart and relationships is vital. Your business is not everyone's business. When we share too much information about our difficulties, we demonstrate a lack of maturity and discernment, and we may end up hurting all the parties involved. You deserve to be protected while seeking a solution to your damaged relationship. God will bring specific people into your life to help you overcome your struggles. I encourage you to seek out trustworthy people who do not gossip or stir up anger concerning an offense but are focused on finding a solution that is God-honoring and emotionally healthy. Be true to the truth, friend.

KEY #5: TAKE THREE ACTION STEPS

If you are the injured party, talk to the person who committed the offense and establish three specific actions they can do to help initiate and maintain the process of rebuilding trust. Those action steps will usually be different for each person and situation. For example, if your teenager has broken your trust, you might both agree to your (1) monitoring their phone, (2) establishing curfew rules, and (3) installing tracking software on their electronic devices. If a friend has broken trust by gossiping about you, you might commit to (1) praying together once a week, (2) speaking to one another in love and kindness, and (3) setting guidelines for what will happen if the trust is broken again.

If you cannot trust yourself, you might take actions such as these: (1) seek help and support from respected Christian counselors or other mature believers, (2) establish safeguards for your life, such as removing yourself from toxic relationships and temptations, and (3) replace negative behaviors with positive ones by actively participating in wholesome daily activities and pursuing your dreams and goals. You might take a college class, work to achieve a promotion at work, or engage socially in a safe way.

KEY #6: SEEK HELP, INCLUDING GODLY COUNSEL

Once you have forgiven someone for an offense, it might become difficult for you to remain focused on the solution or come to a consensus with the other person on how to move forward together. When you are stuck, cannot find your footing, or keep bringing up the individual's offense or other past wrongs, this is a good time to seek the advice and wisdom of a godly counselor. If you are married to the person who has offended you, seek biblically based guidance that will promote unity between you and provide practical steps for navigating your relationship on a daily basis. The following verses from Proverbs encourage us in this wise step: *"Where there is no guidance, a people falls, but in an abundance of counselors there is safety"* (Proverbs 11:14 ESV). *"Plans fail for lack of counsel, but with many advisers they succeed"* (Proverbs 15:22 NIV).

When we exercise true forgiveness, we don't keep a record of wrongs (see 1 Corinthians 13:5), but we do need a plan of action to move forward successfully toward healing and restoration. A godly counselor can help you to develop such a plan. After you establish this plan with the other party, give them a chance to live out their repentance by showing they have changed, demonstrating the transformation that is at work in their lives.

Let me emphasize again that this process will take time. When trust between two people in a relationship has been broken, both parties must examine themselves, acknowledge their wrongs, and commit to solutions that will help rebuild that trust. If the other person is unwilling to follow a plan of restoration, then still consult godly counsel yourself and keep moving forward while surrendering the other person to God. Let go, let God, and continue your own journey to freedom.

ON BECOMING TRUSTWORTHY

In this chapter, we've primarily talked about ways to rebuild trust when someone has broken faith with us in some way. But what if *we're* the one who has done wrong? What can we do to safeguard our destinies from our own damaging ways? "God, save me from myself. Save me from my character defects and my own stony heart"—this was my prayer once upon a time. Let me suggest two ways for you to develop trustworthiness: cultivate godly character and safeguard all your relationships.

CULTIVATE GODLY CHARACTER

It's easy to point an accusing finger at someone who has hurt us. We can dialogue, in detail, about what is wrong with them and how they wounded us. We can express our colorful thoughts and feelings about that person. But the Bible gives us great advice about the order in which God's power works best: *"Why do you look at the speck of sawdust in your brother's eye and pay no attention to the plank in your own eye?... First take the plank out of your own eye, and then you will see clearly to remove the speck from your brother's eye"* (Matthew 7:3, 5 NIV). In other words, we must take the focus off others so we can first examine ourselves and acknowledge where *we* need to change. We need to look inward before looking outward. God will not heal and empower us if we continue to run right back into the mess He is trying to rescue us from, or if we refuse to take the steps to move forward that He is continually placing before us.

In my situation, I took the first step of forgiveness, releasing all the people who had harmed me in the past. I also released myself into the hands of God for all the damage I had caused others. Then, I took the next step and asked God to make me trustworthy—a woman not just of faith but also of character and integrity, someone who could be relied on to follow through with her commitments to herself and others.

This brings us back to the time when I had to sign over the custody of my children. My sons could not be entrusted to my care because of my wounded heart, my rebellion against God, my lack of Christlike character, and the consequences stemming from my addictions. My desire to love them was not enough. I needed to be committed, whole, and healed. Becoming trustworthy meant developing Christlike character.

When we yield to the Holy Spirit, He enables us to cultivate sound character, molding us into the image of Christ as we study God's Word and put it into practice. Our trustworthiness is strengthened with each victory we win over the trials and temptations we face. We will never stop encountering difficulties in this life. (See John 16:33.) However, we can become equipped, through our transformed character, to overcome them. Thus, as we seek to regain integrity in our lives and earn the trust of others, we must develop and follow a strategic plan to overcome the pain, temptations, testings, and trials of life. Victory is not the absence of pain and hardships. Victory is responding constructively to pain and hardships, and standing firm in the midst of them.

Here is the heart of the matter: we become consistent by *doing the right thing over and over again*. In time, we develop trustworthiness and dependability.

When I was learning to be trustworthy, I discovered this wonderful list of godly characteristics to cultivate: *"But the Holy Spirit produces this kind of fruit in our lives: love, joy, peace, patience, kindness, goodness, faithfulness, gentleness, and self-control"* (Galatians 5:22–23 NLT). I asked the Holy Spirit to produce each one of these traits in me and to give me the courage to live them out in times of testing. I prayed for love to replace lust. I prayed for joy to replace despair. Part of my obedience was to come out of isolation and to position myself around joyful people. I prayed for peace to replace my hostility and lack of patience. And I practiced holding my tongue when I was tempted to lash out.

Where life was passing me by, and my dreams and goals lay dormant, I prayed for discipline to shake off my complacency and pursue productivity and achievement. I enrolled in college courses (business and ministry), took up a hobby, and made new friends. I sat down with a professional adviser and drew up a business plan that would enable me to accomplish a dream God had placed in my heart. My dream was to help people and, at the same time, own multiple rental properties. Both of those dreams are now reality. Early in 2022, I bought my second rental property. I also write recovery curriculum, speak all over the world, and offer online courses. I got busy pouring my energies into production instead of wallowing in passivity and sorrow. The passage in Galatians about the fruit of the Spirit taught me which qualities to develop, which characteristics to look for in others, and how to become all that God designed me to be.

Let me caution you that when you're in the midst of building godly character and praying for patience and peace, the temptation to react to negative situations and other people in a hostile way is sure to come. Don't give up. Be alert for times when this happens, and tap into the power of the Holy Spirit so you can respond according to God's way. Become a peacemaker. Take a breath before you say or do anything. Instead of fighting to be right or reacting in a dysfunctional manner, excuse yourself from a negative or antagonistic situation. When you are tempted to lust, flee from that temptation—shut it down. Embrace joy instead of depression. Don't isolate yourself; instead, do something fun with family members or friends. Good character is cultivated in all these ways.

As you build strong character and become trustworthy, you will respond differently, speak differently, and act differently. You will intentionally live in a new, positive, and God-honoring way. By doing this, you will promote the healing process in your life.

WE BECOME CONSISTENT BY DOING THE RIGHT THING OVER AND OVER AGAIN. IN TIME, WE DEVELOP TRUSTWORTHINESS AND DEPENDABILITY.

SAFEGUARD YOURSELF AND YOUR RELATIONSHIPS

When God began to change my character, I had to learn how to guard my heart from entering into relationships that contradicted His Word. When you are not yet healed and have defective character, you can't trust yourself. You don't know how to set boundaries or stand up for yourself. You don't know how to keep yourself safe from making unhealthy decisions or entering into dysfunctional relationships.

Being trustworthy, therefore, includes being aware of, and discerning about, the company we keep. As we have clearly seen, our relationships inevitably influence our lives in either positive or negative ways. The following are some Scriptures that will help you to become judicious in the area of relationships:

+ *"Do not be misled: 'Bad company corrupts good character'"* (1 Corinthians 15:33 NIV). If you compare this verse across multiple Bible versions, you'll see that evil company is described as corrupting *"good character," "good habits," "good morals,"* and *"good manners."*

+ *"Do not make friends with a hot-tempered person, do not associate with one easily angered, or you may learn their ways and get yourself ensnared"* (Proverbs 22:24–25 NIV).

+ *"A gossip goes around telling secrets, so don't hang around with chatter-ers"* (Proverbs 20:19 NLT).

+ *"Don't team up with those who are unbelievers. How can righteous-ness be a partner with wickedness? How can light live with darkness?"* (2 Corinthians 6:14 NLT).

God is a good and gracious Father who has our best interests at heart. He gives us clear direction for protecting ourselves from being hurt or harmed. He knows the powerful influence other people can have on our lives. We begin to emulate those with whom we closely associate. Good or bad, we adopt the characteristics, the ways of thinking, and even the habits and actions of those with whom we spend the most time. For instance, at one point, I realized I was losing my dreams by living with someone who didn't care about his dreams. My behaviors were changing for the better, but I also had to live the life God had called me to. Therefore, it's not only about reforming our bad behavior but also about not allowing our lives to pass us by, because that will cause us—and others—additional hurt and loss.

Let's now consider what we can expect from having close, healthy rela-tionships with godly people. The following Scriptures are a good starting point:

+ *"As iron sharpens iron, so a friend sharpens a friend"* (Proverbs 27:17 NLT).

+ *"The path of life leads upward for the prudent [wise] to keep them from going down to the realm of the dead"* (Proverbs 15:24 NIV).

+ *"The godly offer good counsel; they teach right from wrong. They have made God's law their own, so they will never slip from his path"* (Psalm 37:30–31 NLT).

Using the Bible's wisdom as your reference point, examine your various relationships. Being honest about your interactions with others will help you understand how to establish and promote good relationships in your life while navigating difficult relationships. After prioritizing time with your spouse and family, you have the power to decide, for better or worse, who to invest your energies in and who to spend time with. When I heeded the above Scriptures and established powerful and positive friendships, I became hungry for joy, spiritual and personal growth, and success in various areas of my life. I was intentional about keeping company with strong, joyful, and successful Christian women. Their positive qualities were contagious. I started dreaming great, God-given dreams—and pursuing them with passion!

As you evaluate each of your friendships and/or dating relationships, ask yourself the following questions:

- Am I always pouring affection, respect, concern, and care into the relationship without the other person reciprocating?

- Does my romantic partner hold the same beliefs that I hold?

- Does my friend or romantic partner challenge me to grow in my walk with Christ, or do they tempt me to compromise my beliefs?

- Is this friendship based on healthy boundaries, growth, and activities?

- Does my friend encourage me to become the very best I can be in life? Do they build me up spiritually in Christ? Do they give me sound advice? Do they invite me to have fun without compromising my standards?

Relationships that are not of God will rob you of joy and confidence. They will pull you away from His plan for your life. You will not be able to see the doors of favor and promise that God has opened for you if you are chasing wrong or misguided pursuits. Choosing the right people with whom to share your life can be a difficult challenge, but it is a process that will keep you on the path to freedom and enable you to stay aligned with God's very best for you. The right people will encourage and challenge you to establish healthy, powerful goals.

If you do not yet have positive friendships such as I have just described, pray that the Lord will establish strong, godly relationships in your life. Ask Him to put the right people in your path. He will do it. But you need to do your part. You must be intentional about it. Go to places where godly people are present. Don't just attend church on Sunday mornings but also become involved in the life of the congregation during the week. You can join a prayer group or Bible study, volunteer to serve others, and gather at social events with like-minded and spiritually sound people. Positioning yourself to meet the people God wants to connect you with will set you on the road to great favor and genuine love. Friend, fight for yourself and your newfound freedom. Freedom doesn't happen by chance. It happens by choice and by deliberate participation.

TRUST GOD—ALWAYS

Regardless of who has broken your heart or your trust, remember that the Bible assures us God is always trustworthy. Let's return to what I think is one of the greatest pieces of advice we could ever take: *"Trust in the LORD with all your heart, and lean not on your own understanding; in all your ways acknowledge Him, and He shall direct your paths"* (Proverbs 3:5–6 NKJV). Why should you trust God? Because you can count on Him. He's the only One who will never break faith with you. He's the holder of your heart. He will protect your heart, care for it, treasure it, and keep it safe in His custody.

You can completely trust in God's character and integrity. He will never leave you or forsake you. (See, for example, Deuteronomy 31:6; Hebrews 13:5–6.) He wants nothing but the best for you! And He will guide you in the ways of rebuilding trust, developing godly character, and safeguarding your relationships. He will heal your heart and set your feet on solid ground so you can move past all offenses and enter into the abundant life He has prepared for you.

He is the Rock; his deeds are perfect. Everything he does is just and fair. He is a faithful God who does no wrong; how just and upright he is! (Deuteronomy 32:4 NLT)

COURAGE CHOICES FOR YOUR HEALING

1. If you are in a situation where healing needs to take place and trust needs to be rebuilt, what are some steps you can take to begin the healing process and move forward in the life God has for you? Here are some examples:

    a. Forgiving everyone who has wronged you. If you have not yet taken this step, remember that you need to forgive to allow your healing to begin and to experience the fullness of freedom Jesus offers you.

    b. Establishing healthy boundaries. If you have not yet determined those boundaries, make a list of healthy boundaries you can establish to safeguard your heart and life.

    c. Seeking godly counsel to help you move forward in the healing process and in your life. Remember, there is no shame in seeking counsel. We all need godly counsel in life. Get the help you need.

2. As you evaluate each of your friendships and/or dating relationships, ask yourself the following questions:

    a. Am I always pouring affection, respect, concern, and care into the relationship without the other person reciprocating?

    b. Does my romantic partner hold the same beliefs that I hold?

c. Does my friend or romantic partner challenge me to grow in my walk with Christ, or do they tempt me to compromise my beliefs?

d. Is this friendship based on healthy boundaries, growth, and activities?

e. Does my friend encourage me to become the very best I can be in life? Do they build me up spiritually in Christ? Do they give me sound advice? Do they invite me to have fun without compromising my standards?

3. Write out all the Scripture passages from the section entitled "Safeguard Yourself and Your Relationships" that help to define unhealthy and healthy people-connections.

4. Consider the people-connections in your life:

a. List the names of several people with whom you have healthy relationships. What makes those relationships healthy?

b. List the names of the people with whom you have unhealthy relationships that God is telling you to let go of. What makes those relationships unhealthy?

c. Where can you position yourself to develop godly relation-ships with others? Remember, we cannot isolate ourselves or put ourselves in dark, compromising situations and expect healthy, godly relationships to materialize.

5. Is there a dream God has placed in your heart that has been delayed because of your negative habits, your past, or your pain?

a. Write down what that dream is.

b. Now make a courage choice to pray and ask God how He would like you to begin taking action steps for realizing the dream He has given you. You're worth it, friend!

6

SETTING HEALTHY BOUNDARIES

If you need to forgive someone who is close to you—such as a spouse or another family member—for an offense or a betrayal, it can be difficult to rebuild trust with them if they continue to engage in dysfunctional behaviors. Once you have forgiven them, it will be necessary for you to put healthy boundaries in place while the healing process continues.

I previously mentioned that when Darryl and I first got married, he reopened the door to some old friends and fell back into destructive habits for some time. He was no longer a faithful husband, and he struggled with his addictions. Once again, it seemed that, every week, there was another woman, another betrayal, another excuse, another apology. But, now that we were married, I couldn't just pack my bags and leave. I learned how to love Darryl and not leave him, without losing myself. How did I do this? I set firm boundaries, remained faithful to him, kept praying and standing in faith, and continued living my life with purpose and power.

"THINGS WILL BE DIFFERENT THIS TIME"

Darryl had fallen away from the Lord over time. I knew that meant the old stony, stubborn heart would resurface. Friend, this is why I emphasize safeguarding your life at all times. Compromise is always waiting for you to succumb to it. You are at risk of bottoming out in life any time you open yourself up to old, negative ways of living. That includes keeping company with people who exert an unhealthy influence on you. Let me warn you that the damages and heartaches are not worth risking a relapse. One of the meanings of the word *relapse* is "to fall or slip back into a former state, practice. etc."[5] This definition does not specifically mention falling back into drugs or alcohol. The word is not just a recovery term. Are you currently in danger of relapsing, or returning to a negative pattern, way of coping, or relationship? Permanently reject any thoughts of turning back to what has defeated you in the past, whatever or whoever it may be. Forge forward in God's ways!

At the beginning of this period of our marriage, Darryl and I would fight often—and we frequently fought dirty. I would yell and even throw things at him. He would hurl back hurtful insults and then walk away as if he didn't even care. It was an extremely painful time—and that's putting it mildly. A few days after a fight, Darryl would approach me and say two words I came to dread: "I'm sorry." I use the word *dread* because I knew the phrase meant nothing to him. His repeated apologies and promises to change rang hollow. Darryl was stuck in a cycle of sin.

As I mentioned in the previous chapter, a person who is stuck in this type of cycle may make promises such as these:

+ "I'm so sorry. I'll never do it again!"

+ "I promise that I'll change."

+ "Things will be different this time."

Again, the individual may mean the words at the time, but if they never truly surrender to the power of God or participate in the process of change, the behavior will present itself once again. As the empty promises keep coming, the person on the receiving end experiences a roller coaster of emotions, from daring to be hopeful for change to being devastated by a lack of follow-through on the part of their loved one or friend. And, each time the promises prove to be empty, the wound of offense is reopened.

After saying he was sorry, Darryl would wonder why I stayed quiet or refused to be intimate with him. He'd pester me about it until I would get so frustrated that I would start screaming at him all over again.

---

5. *Dictionary.com*, s.v. "relapse," https://www.dictionary.com/browse/relapse.

"But you said you forgave me. What's the problem?" Darryl would ask.

While he was right that I had forgiven him, I was also deeply wounded. I finally said to him, "I forgive you, but I do not trust you, and I need time to heal!" That got his attention. I expressed to him the process I described in the previous chapter: once trust is broken, it needs to be rebuilt, and healing needs to take place. All that requires time. Forgiving him was the immediate part. Have you been able to grasp the difference between forgiveness being immediate and the process of healing and rebuilding trust being the journey that requires time and work? I had to learn how to love Darryl while safeguarding my heart and my God-given destiny.

It is important to mention here that Darryl had experienced major traumas in his life that had harmed him deeply, and he had never gone through a process of healing with the Holy Spirit. When such wounds are not placed into the hands of the Healer, they will devour and even destroy you, along with anyone you try to love. An unhealed heart is dangerous and desperate. Unless you seek healing, you will make those whom you love pay for your past without even realizing it is happening. This was my condition before I gave my life to Christ and experienced the life-transforming and healing power of God you are reading about in this book! Unhealed wounds and offenses produce pain that leaves pathways of destruction, just as a Category 5 hurricane destroys everything in its path. They keep you bound to destructive behaviors and dysfunctional living and loving, producing repetitive cycles of defeat.

A person who is entrenched in dysfunction is stuck in unhealthy, sinful, or destructive patterns—refusing to change. Instead of repenting by turning away from their sin and turning toward God, they repeatedly go back to their sinful outlook and behavior. When a loved one or friend continually says they are sorry without ever correcting their attitudes and behaviors, the only way to safeguard your heart is to set boundaries for yourself that will protect you and them. This prevents you from losing yourself and from enabling the harmful behavior. Restoration is not always guaranteed, as I indicated earlier, but we can trust God to take control of the situation as we yield it to Him. Let me encourage you that you can move forward even if the person you love chooses to remain stuck. Keep trusting God, friend. Keep moving forward in Him.

Are you the person on the receiving end of betrayal, or are you the perpetrator of it? I've shared both sides of my story—times when I was the one doing wrong, and times when I was wronged. Both types of situations need to be rectified. Honesty about such matters is essential if change is to occur. When you and your loved one are intentional about following the principles in this book, it will lead you both into healing that results in true freedom.

So, how do you forgive and show love to an offender without losing your self-respect and becoming a doormat? In the next section, I offer some guidelines for setting healthy boundaries—rules or promises that have consequences when broken. Depending on the situation, setting boundaries can either work alongside of, or precede, the keys I described in the previous chapter for rebuilding trust, including establishing three action steps for the person to follow in order to demonstrate their changed behavior.

> **WHEN YOU AND YOUR LOVED ONE ARE INTENTIONAL ABOUT FOLLOWING THE PRINCIPLES IN THIS BOOK, IT WILL LEAD YOU BOTH INTO HEALING THAT RESULTS IN TRUE FREEDOM.**

THE POWER OF SETTING BOUNDARIES

When I understood that I was experiencing emotional pain because I still needed to heal from the effects of Darryl's unfaithfulness and dysfunctional behavior, I made a choice to guard my heart while trusting God for my restoration and the renewal of our marriage. I had to draw a line in the sand. I told Darryl I loved him with every fiber of my being. Again, the issue wasn't love; it was trust. You can love another person dearly and still not trust them. You can even love God but show you don't really trust Him by rejecting His ways of doing things. I told Darryl I was standing in faith that God would work a miracle in our marriage. But, I also told him that, in the meantime, I had to establish strong boundaries that would be challenging for both of us to hold to.

MAKE THE BOUNDARIES CLEAR AND SPECIFIC

First, it's important to make the boundaries clear and specific so they can be carefully followed. For example, I told Darryl we were not going to share our marriage bed until he stopped being unfaithful to me. For one thing, I wasn't going to subject myself to the possibility of contracting a sexually transmitted disease. Neither was I going to damage my soul by giving in to his desires for physical pleasure while I was suffering emotionally. I needed to protect my body, my mind, my heart, my soul, and my spirit. So, I set this boundary: Darryl had to move into another bedroom in the house.

I also explained to him that I was going to open my own bank account to safeguard our finances because they were dwindling rapidly as he used our money to feed his addictions and was otherwise careless about his spending. I was not hiding anything from Darryl, nor was I taking the money to use it on myself. I was safeguarding my marriage for the future by being responsible to ensure that our bills were paid and our financial security remained intact.

Finally, I told Darryl I refused to participate in explosive arguments any longer. If he spoke to me disrespectfully or in anger, I would walk away from the conversation.

STOP DWELLING ON THE SITUATION AND SURRENDER IT TO GOD

Before our marriage, I had been in the same place with Darryl. Therefore, I knew how to respond to the situation from a godly perspective because I had previously implemented principles for healing that included boundaries. The main response I needed to make was to surrender myself and Darryl completely over to God. What did that mean? It meant preparing for the worst while standing in faith for the best. I was realistic and yet believed that God would do great things. I continued loving Darryl within the firm boundaries I had set. I also stopped obsessing over his behavior and ceased trying to change him. That meant I refrained from cleaning up his messes and left him to answer for himself and face his own consequences. I put everything—our lives, our marriage, my wounded heart, Darryl's dysfunctional habits, and our future—in God's hands. Rather than feeling powerless over the situation, I made room for the power of God to work in my life and in Darryl's life.

MOVE FORWARD WITH YOUR OWN LIFE

Once I fully committed the situation to God, I no longer retreated from my own life or from working toward the success of my dreams and goals. I diligently pursued my real estate career, continued my divinity classes online, and faithfully attended church, Bible studies, and prayer meetings. I kept going and growing, refusing to allow the enemy to steal another day of my life or another moment of my joy, even in the midst of my pain and tears. When I chose to live in victory, the pain lessened because I didn't feel powerless or overwhelmed with fear over a possible negative outcome. The tears became fewer and fewer because I embraced my self-worth and refused to be devalued or defeated.

Friend, when you choose victory for yourself, you also choose victory for your loved ones by default. Our choices and actions affect everyone around us. I knew God would take care of me regardless of the outcome. As I entrusted the situation to God, I kept busy building my own life. I became empowered while waiting for a miracle in my marriage and for breakthroughs in the lives of my children. If my husband wasn't going to change, I still had the power to do so. I put myself in a position where God could move in my life even if Darryl chose not to heal and grow.

I didn't turn my attention to another man who could "complete me," default to complaining in chat rooms, or indulge in depressing thoughts of what "should be." I made what *was* count!

I did not allow sorrow, depression, or defeat to win the day, the week, or the year. I got up and stayed up!

I grew stronger and stronger as I lived my life for Jesus. I focused on the abilities God had given me instead of what I wasn't receiving from Darryl or from anyone or anything else. I made the choice to become fully alive in the midst of a dead situation. As a result, I became resilient, free, and successful. I was proud of my progress and grateful for the ways God was working in my life.

Are you getting this, my friend? I was going to live a full life for Christ regardless of my circumstances or the difficulties in my relationships and their potential outcomes. And that is exactly what happened.

WHEN YOU CHOOSE VICTORY FOR YOURSELF, YOU ALSO CHOOSE VICTORY FOR YOUR LOVED ONES BY DEFAULT. OUR CHOICES AND ACTIONS AFFECT EVERYONE AROUND US.

STICK TO THE BOUNDARIES YOU HAVE SET

After establishing healthy boundaries, we must be careful to stick to them. Whenever times were tough, temptation arose, or I wanted to quit, I was determined not to give in or isolate myself from others. Instead, I picked up the phone and called strong Christian friends for prayer and encouragement. I intentionally attended my Christ-centered support groups and sought godly counseling. With deliberate steps, I walked through the pain. And, as I walked, I found fun, hope, and joy in Christ, in my family and friends, and in my continued growth and achievements.

SAFEGUARDING OUR HEARTS AND LIVES

I set in place those drastic boundaries with Darryl to ensure my well-being. It was not an easy process, and he did not change immediately. In fact, it took about two years before our marriage was truly reconciled. However, what did change along the way was me. As I sought God with vigilance and desperation, He began to work on my character. I was no longer the wild, reactive wife. I no longer begged for Darryl's attention. I no longer acted like an obsessed "detective," snooping through all of Darryl's belongings for evidence of affairs or drug use. And I no longer stalked him with phone calls.

Not only did I establish boundaries with my husband, but I also set one additional boundary for myself. I asked the Lord to become the guard of my mouth. I had a bad habit of talking to Darryl in a disrespectful way. I was harsh. I was snarky. I used words to insult him instead of speaking the truth in love to him and allowing God's truth to change him.

As I gave the situation to God and began to heal, I learned to take a stand for myself and be firm in my speech without being foolish, irrational, reactive, or dishonoring. This was a miraculous change in me! The Holy Spirit delivered me from my disrespectful mouth as He healed my broken heart. I would no longer attack Darryl with my words or hurl objects at him during heated arguments. I stuck to my boundaries and held my peace. Through God's power, I was enabled to rise above my circumstances and experience His peace that *"transcends all understanding."* (See Philippians 4:6–7.)

Over time, Darryl noticed the changes in me, and, ultimately, he recommitted his life to Jesus. He has remained faithful to Christ, to me, and to our family ever since. He cut ties with the old friends who had led him back into his dysfunctional behavior and addictions. He stopped going to the places where he was tempted to fall away from God. How was he was able to do that? Through the transforming power of God's Word and the strength of the Holy Spirit. Darryl also formed relationships with godly men through which he could receive support and grow spiritually. When he was tempted to go back to his old ways, he picked up the phone and called those men, and they helped him stay the course. He safeguarded his life. This, in turn, protected our marriage and helped to heal our relationship.

Now, Darryl and I share a message of healing and restoration around the world to help others overcome the same obstacles. He is one of the most powerful men of God that I know, as well as an amazing husband and father. I love him beyond words! I'm so grateful that we serve the God of the impossible. All things are possible with God when we do it His way!

A PATTERN OF PRINCIPLES FOR ANY DIFFICULTY

I want you to notice a pattern of principles in the above points. The steps I had embraced to gain my personal freedom are the same steps I used for the healing of my marriage and my relationships with my children. I established healthy boundaries for myself and others, focused on making courageous choices and following through with them, walked according to the freedom I gained each day, and lived in a continual state of breakthrough!

I have unfolded this pathway to freedom on every page of *The Courage to Heal.* It comes down to making positive choices, based on biblical principles, that require courage and gut-wrenching honesty but result in real healing and newness of life. The principles that set me free still keep me free to this very day. I have applied the same principles to every difficult situation I have faced since committing my life to Christ. The principles worked when I lost custody of my sons, when my mother passed away, and when I experienced financial devastation. The principles worked throughout the Covid-19 pandemic and all its challenges.

The principles worked when one of my children fell into addiction. At times, he would be homeless or missing for months without a word, and I didn't know if he was dead or alive. For years, I applied these principles as I trusted God to help him overcome his addiction. The principles were successful because I kept using them and never gave up.

These principles of healing and restoration will work when life seems to be going well, and you are happy, and they will also work when troubles and trials show up with a vengeance. Whatever troubles you face, you have the choice to become free and remain free all the days of your life. You are worth it, friend!

HEALING AND BOUNDARIES

Healing and boundaries go hand in hand. Boundaries are guidelines and action steps that must be developed with careful consideration, thought, and planning. Their purpose is to protect your heart and the healing work God is doing in your life. They empower you to become fully alive, even in the midst of a painful or dead relationship. They equip you to move forward through the most challenging of circumstances.

Setting boundaries is never easy. Remember Proverbs 4:23, which talks about the need to guard your heart? Think of a boundary as a guard. It is meant to defend you. When you set boundaries and enforce them, you reclaim your power and regain control over your own life even when your loved one is living a destructive, dysfunctional lifestyle.

The boundaries I established not only safeguarded my heart, but they also got Darryl's attention. I want to make clear that I did not set those boundaries as a manipulative strategy to get him to change. I knew better. I was strong enough in my faith to understand that only God could change Darryl, if he was willing to surrender to Him. And, once again, God used my example of obedience to Him to show Darryl what a life sold out to

Jesus looks like. Little did I know that, through my daily example, Darryl was experiencing God's grace and love while I was experiencing His supernatural power to persevere in faith, hope, and love. I was drawing my identity completely from Christ, and Darryl could see the difference in me. Through my actions, and not my words, the Holy Spirit convicted Darryl to turn from his sin yet again. Eventually, this promise from God found in 1 Peter 3:1–2 came to fruition: *"Even if some refuse to obey the Good News, your godly lives will speak to them without any words. They will be won over by observing your pure and reverent lives"* (NLT).

> **BOUNDARIES ARE GUIDELINES AND ACTION STEPS THAT MUST BE DEVELOPED WITH CAREFUL CONSIDERATION, THOUGHT, AND PLANNING. THEIR PURPOSE IS TO PROTECT YOUR HEART AND THE HEALING WORK GOD IS DOING IN YOUR LIFE.**

I must say it again: today, Darryl is one of the most loving and powerful men of God that I know. One demonstration of his healing and transformation was the way he prayed for me regarding my trauma from the rape attack. He prayed with spiritual authority over that situation not long after he recommitted his life to Christ. What a difference Jesus makes in life and in love when we follow His ways and allow Him to work His purposes in us! Now, Darryl and I both travel the nation and the world evangelizing and teaching for the Lord. We also share how God healed each of us from our brokenness and restored our marriage. Not only do we serve alongside one another in ministry, but we are also more in love with each other than ever before. Our journey to freedom came alive for us as we accepted God's forgiveness, forgave one another, received God's healing, established healthy boundaries, and rebuilt trust between us—it came alive as we *lived* God's way.

It is our hope that our victory in Christ will help to bring healing to multitudes of people around the world who struggle with many of the same issues we did. We continue to have the awesome privilege of seeing many lives transformed and many marriages saved. As it was for us, we believe your best is yet to come, friend!

You can make the choice to enter into the journey to freedom even if your loved one—whether it is your spouse, child, parent, or friend—does not choose to do so. No one and nothing can delay your freedom in Christ except you. Freedom is always a choice. Even if a situation does not change, you can change, and you can set healthy boundaries for yourself and others. You do not have to stay stuck, hopeless, or fearful. You can move forward in God's purpose and plan for your life. God has given me the strength and courage to stand my ground throughout all the struggles of my life, and He's got your back as well. Stay encouraged as we continue on the pathway to healing.

COURAGE CHOICES FOR YOUR HEALING

1. What behaviors or patterns are you exhibiting that are harming yourself, your relationships, your goals, your dreams, and/or your ability to live successfully each day?

2. Do you feel like you are losing yourself while waiting for a loved one to find themself? If so, what boundaries can you set to safeguard your heart and begin to heal?

3. What steps can you take to find yourself once again?

4. What steps can you take to purposefully pursue joy and become joyful once more?

5. How can you become fully alive amid a dead situation or circumstance?

Friend, you were not meant to live lost. Get going with God, your destiny, and your future!

7

A GOD-DESIGNED
HEART TRANSPLANT

We've covered a lot of ground so far—transformative concepts like receiving and releasing forgiveness, rebuilding trust, and establishing boundaries. It is my prayer that your courage to heal is growing as you read this book. Jesus Christ, the Son of God, wants you to have a spiritually healthy heart and a transformed life. This is possible for anyone who is willing to surrender to His healing work. In this chapter, I want to bring the various aspects of the healing process together, reviewing them through an illustrative lens—that of a heart transplant.

WITNESSING OPEN-HEART SURGERY

Soon after I graduated from high school, I made a decision to go to nursing school. I have always desired to help others, even during my darkest days, and I felt that nursing would be a wonderful vocation. I never finished my nurse's training program because I chose to marry at the young age of twenty. However, I learned a tremendous amount about medicine and healing during the time I spent in the program, and it has remained with me. I have applied many of the principles I learned to my spiritual and emotional healing.

After I was accepted into the nursing program, as part of my training, I worked on the telemetry floor of the hospital to which I had been assigned. This was a specific area for patients with heart defects. There, I helped to monitor patients' hearts and collect data so the doctors could do further analysis and provide the best treatment.

One glorious day, I was offered what I felt was the opportunity of a lifetime: to be present in the operating room to witness open-heart surgery. I had never seen anything like it before, nor have I seen anything like it since. This high-stakes surgery is extremely invasive and gravely consequential, yet it is often a critical procedure for saving a patient's life.

The medical team meticulously scrubs up to ensure they are free of any germs, and the patient is prepped for the surgery. The eyes and ears of all the medical staff in the operating room are on the mighty surgeon as they await his every command, which must be followed with precise movement, detail, and timing. There is no room for error or indecision.

In order to reach the patient's heart, their sternum must be broken and then held open by two claws of steel, giving room and visibility for the surgeon to perform his life-saving work. I was in awe at seeing the human body so exposed and vulnerable as I witnessed this delicate yet powerful work.

OUR GREAT PHYSICIAN

Later, when I was experiencing deep spiritual and emotional healing in my life, this vivid picture of the operating room—as well as the intensive care unit and the surgeon's instructions for the recovery process—became a beautiful analogy for me of how God heals us from the deepest, darkest wounds and defects we experience in life. Likewise, I pray that the following analogy of a heart transplant may help you to fully grasp the process of becoming new as you overcome what has defeated you and caused you pain in the past. We will review all the steps we've covered thus far to highlight the chronological progression of this experiential process that enables us to become healthy and healed under the mighty hand of Jesus, the Great Physician, who is also our Heart Surgeon.

Imagine you have a physical heart ailment, and, although you are not yet aware of it, you will need a heart transplant. You are rushed to the emergency room with severe chest pains. Your heart is deeply damaged and not functioning properly. As soon as you enter the hospital, you are surrounded by a team of doctors and nurses who begin asking you questions such as the following as they assess the problem:

+ "When did the pain start?"

+ "On a scale of one to ten, how bad is your pain?"

+ "What were you doing when the pain started?"

+ "Has this happened before?"

+ "Tell me about your medical history."

+ "Have you had prior surgeries?"

The medical team members have one thing on their minds: to save your life and to help heal whatever needs to be healed. Each doctor and nurse attending to you is assigned a specific task. Their collective goal is to stabilize your heart rate, as well as your blood pressure and oxygen level, while gathering every bit of information possible to determine the best treatment plan for you. The doctors determine that your heart condition is so serious that a transplant is required. Reality check: Jesus desires to do the same for us spiritually. Our heart condition, due to our sin and the fallen world in which we live, is such that we need Him to give us a brand-new heart.

PRE-SURGERY CONSENT AND CHECKLIST

A heart donation becomes available for you, and your transplant surgery is quickly scheduled. Before the surgery takes place, you are asked to sign a consent form. This gives the hospital permission to treat you. By signing on the dotted line, you agree to the surgery and your cardiologist's treatment plan; you relinquish all control of your life into the medical team's hands. But, as we will see, simply signing the consent form for treatment will not make you well. You will have to submit to the whole process—not just the surgery but also everything else that is needed for a full recovery.

The spiritual equivalent of the consent form is to surrender your past, present, and future into the hands of the Great Physician, who desires to make you well. You obey Jesus's command to forgive. You no longer hold your offenders in contempt but instead release them and their offenses to God. You relinquish any notion of vengeance or claim to justice. You forfeit your position as jury, judge, and executioner. If you do not agree to these conditions of surrender, the Great Physician cannot perform your heart transplant.

It's important to note that many people languish spiritually for the following two reasons. First, although they believe in Jesus, they refuse to forgive themselves or others. But we have seen that forgiveness is not optional. It's a command. The process of spiritual and emotional healing begins with receiving forgiveness from God. Forgiveness is the gateway, the entryway, to being made whole. Without forgiveness, we cannot exchange our hearts for God's heart. Second, as I mentioned earlier, people often think that all they have to do is say a magical phrase like "I forgive so-and-so," and everything will go back to "normal." But, again, the healing journey includes practices like releasing vengeance over to the Lord, reexamining our own attitudes and the nature of all our relationships, and establishing healthy boundaries when needed.

Before a heart surgeon makes the first incision in a patient's chest, the medical team cleans the area of all impurities in order to prevent infection. Spiritually speaking, forgiveness is the cleansing agent that allows us to receive the finished work of Jesus Christ. When we ask Jesus to forgive us and all who have harmed us, we are now ready and positioned to receive our new hearts. Jesus Christ, the Great Physician, can go to work, and the healing process can continue after the heart transplant takes place.

Give God permission to do His work in your heart. Let the finished work of the cross begin transforming you on the inside by eradicating the sinful impurities and harmful effects of life so the Great Physician can replace your heart of stone with a heart that is tender toward Him, one that can love right and live right. *"I will give you a new heart, and I will put a new spirit in you. I will take out your stony, stubborn heart and give you a tender, responsive heart"* (Ezekiel 36:26 NLT).

Once you have surrendered your pain, sin, past, and present to Jesus Christ, He cleanses you from every sin, wrong, harm, and hurt. You are now ready to undergo the life-changing operation in which His miraculous work will be performed.

YOUR HEART-SURGERY TEAM

During your heart-transplant surgery, a team of people surrounds you at all times. The team consists of well-equipped doctors, nurses, and other medical personnel to whom you have entrusted your care. You will never be left alone throughout the operation or during the recovery process in the hospital. Likewise, Jesus never intended us to walk through life and our healing journeys by ourselves. None of us can travel our journey alone. God will place specific people in your path to help you along the road to healing and freedom. Keep your eyes, ears, and heart open for those moments when He has ordained you to interact with someone who will encourage, challenge, or motivate you when you need it most. I like to call these moments "God encounters." The most likely place to have a God encounter is among other believers. The church is not a building or a Sunday service that you attend for an hour or two each week. The church is the whole body of Christ, and each of us needs to be a member of a local fellowship of Christians where we can be spiritually nurtured and serve others.

In the past, you may have been hurt by a fellow church member or even a church leader, and, for this reason, you may be wary of participating in a local congregation. If so, you are not alone. Many believers have been hurt in this way. Why? Because, like every single person on this planet, churchgoers and church leaders are human. We are all imperfect people. We all sin and make mistakes. But Jesus is the Head of the church, and He is perfectly trustworthy and more than qualified to heal your broken heart. Do not allow a bad religious experience to prevent you from regularly attending services at a Bible-teaching church and becoming involved in the life of the congregation. Forgive those church members or leaders who have hurt you, and establish healthy boundaries in some of those relationships if needed. Ask the Holy Spirit to confirm which local fellowship He wants you to be a part of. Once He does this, I encourage you to attend Bible studies, prayer groups, and church fellowship functions. Serve others using your God-given skills, talents, and abilities. God will use these avenues to bring people into your life who will help you walk the pathway to healing and wholeness.

KEEP YOUR EYES, EARS, AND HEART OPEN FOR THOSE MOMENTS WHEN GOD HAS ORDAINED YOU TO INTERACT WITH SOMEONE WHO WILL ENCOURAGE, CHALLENGE, OR MOTIVATE YOU WHEN YOU NEED IT MOST.

THE SURGERY

When you first arrived at the emergency room with the pain in your chest, you had no idea that you would need a heart transplant, and you had no special knowledge of heart surgeons or who would perform your operation. You were in a desperate situation that demanded you trust the medical personnel at the hospital as you relied on their skills and expertise. Now, as you undergo the heart-transplant surgery, you are under anesthesia and unconscious, and you have to trust the physician and their team who are performing your operation.

Similarly, along your journey to healing and freedom, you must trust God to do what only He can do: heal you from the deepest wounds of your past. Trusting God is essential to the healing process. God will perform the work only if you let Him. But if you trust Him, you will come out of His spiritual surgery with a brand-new heart.

As you lie on the operating table to receive your heart transplant, the surgeon, in order to reach your heart, slices open your chest and breaks your sternum, similar to what I watched the surgeon do when I observed open-heart surgery as a nursing student. Then, the medical team clamps two large metal claws to your sternum to keep it open to make room for the transplant procedure. The surgeon and the team are meticulous as they remove your old heart. Then, the new heart is placed into the surgeon's hands to implant inside your chest cavity. Likewise, Jesus, the Great Physician, works meticulously to ensure that your sin-infected, dysfunctional, broken, and wounded heart is removed.

When you had first arrived at the emergency room with your heart in crisis, you were asked to provide your background and medical history. Thus, your past was exposed to the medical team, enabling them to have a better idea of everything that had negatively affected or harmed the condition of your heart. Spiritually and emotionally speaking, what has negatively affected or harmed your heart for far too long? What has caused you pain for years? What has led to your brokenness? Which memories haunt you? Which regrets shame you? Here is the good news, my friend: God already knows! And He is ready to remove your broken, stony heart and make all things new.

Picture Jesus removing your old heart and implanting within you a new, spiritually healthy one. The heart of God is now inside of you, sewn up and sealed through His Holy Spirit. This new heart can love right and live right. God says, "I will heal your broken heart and bind up your wounds." (See Psalm 147:3). Spiritually, your new heart is ready to beat in a strong way through new experiences, new boundaries, and a new way of life. You are God's new creation. *"Therefore, if anyone is in Christ, the new creation has come: the old has gone, the new is here!"* (2 Corinthians 5:17 NIV). Your motivations, priorities, thoughts, words, and actions are being transformed into the image of Christ as you yield yourself to Him. In order for this miraculous work to take its full effect, a few lifestyle changes will be necessary, starting with establishing a close relationship with God through Jesus Christ.

THE INTENSIVE CARE UNIT

After your heart-transplant surgery, you are moved to the intensive care unit (ICU), a specialized department in the hospital that provides critical care and around-the-clock monitoring in a controlled environment where only specific people are allowed to be around you. Your time in the ICU is vital to your recovery. You are given complete rest, and you are limited in movement so that your body can focus on healing.

The spiritual parallel to the ICU is periods of time spent alone with God during which you pray, read your Bible, and reflect on your life. During these times, consider your habits—where you go and what you do every day. Think about what you need to do differently to protect your heart as you heal. Reevaluate your relationships. Is there anyone with whom you should cut ties? Which relationships will you keep? What new hobbies or lifestyle choices will you embrace? What boundaries must you establish so that God's mighty work is not contaminated during this critical part of your healing process?

REHABILITATION

Finally, you are moved out of the ICU and into a regular hospital room. It's time to begin the process of rehabilitation. A nurse or occupational therapist delivers the great news that you are going to be given the excruciating and exhausting task of sitting up in a chair for a short period of time the first day. Remember, steel claws held open your chest cavity during your surgery. Recovering from that procedure and the operation as a whole will require time and effort.

You begin by merely sitting up in a chair. Then, you progress to moving around your room. Finally, you're ready to walk—slowly and painfully—down the corridor. You get the picture. You must endure the discomfort and pain of sitting up before you can start walking around and eventually be ready to leave the hospital to continue recovering at home. It will take time, help from others, courage, and determination to keep moving forward, pressing through the pain. But, each day, you will gain strength as your new heart continues to acclimate itself to your body, and you progress in your healing.

At times, spiritual and emotional healing can be a very painful process too. Nevertheless, this process is essential, and it cannot be passed over or ignored. It is part of the journey that leads to wholeness. When we acknowledge our sin, confess it to God, release our pain to Him, and give Him our lives, we participate in His process of change. Letting God do His work means handing over to Him whatever He needs to transform in our lives in order to bring about our healing.

Please understand that surrendering our hurts and dysfunctions to God doesn't mean merely praying and asking Him to make everything perfect. We are participants in the rehabilitation process. We have an active role in our healing. We participate by maintaining a relationship with God and obeying His Word. God is a relational Being, and we are meant to be in an ongoing personal relationship with Him. When we partner with God in our healing—and in all aspects of our lives—that's what makes the relationship personal.

A powerful way to partner with God in the healing process is by journaling. If you don't already use a spiritual journal or prayer journal, daily set aside time for solitude, prayer, and self-reflection. Journal your thoughts and prayers. You can use whatever medium you are comfortable with for your journaling, whether it is pen and paper, a tablet, a smartphone, or another tool. As the Bible says, *"Write the vision and make it plain"* (Habakkuk 2:2 NKJV). Your journal is a written account of your experiences with God. It is your testimony of how He is setting you free. If you already practice journaling, great. Keep it up!

Through daily prayer and reflection, ask God to examine your heart and reveal to you any sinful practice, negative attitude, or hurtful memory you may be harboring. This is a vital spiritual discipline to practice in order to guard your heart in the midst of our fallen and sinful world where Satan is constantly trying to steal, kill, and destroy the abundant life God desires for us. (See John 10:10.) During your spiritual heart surgery, the old "you" died, and you were resurrected to new life in Christ with a new heart. As the apostle Paul wrote, *"My old self has been crucified with Christ. It is no longer I who live, but Christ lives in me. So, I live in this earthly body by trusting in the Son of God, who loved me and gave himself for me"* (Galatians 2:20 NLT).

Every day, we can find ourselves in situations where we need to receive forgiveness from God and release forgiveness to others. When we do this, we give God full permission to continually wash us clean. We will mess up. We will make mistakes. People will harm us. We will always need God's forgiveness for ourselves and others. Isaiah 55:7 tells us that if we turn to the Lord and forsake our wicked ways, He will have mercy on us. He will forgive and pardon us.

Thus, when you seek God, confessing your sins and releasing the offenses of those who have caused you harm, you actively contribute to the healing process. Below are some verses from the Bible that reinforce this truth. Meditate on them. Let them soak into your spirit. Say them over and over out loud until they become part of you:

Search me, O God, and know my heart; test me and know my anxious thoughts. Point out anything in me that offends you, and lead me along the path of everlasting life. (Psalm 139:23–24 NLT)

I will cleanse them from all their wickedness (guilt) by which they have sinned against Me, and I will pardon (forgive) all their sins by which they rebelled against Me. (Jeremiah 33:8 AMP)

To continue our surgical analogy, you are finally discharged from the hospital by the doctor, having been given a strategic set of instructions that you must not only read but also apply in order to experience a healthy life. Friend, the spiritual parallel is that a head knowledge of Scripture is not enough. And while a five-minute daily devotional is a good practice for someone who is just learning about Jesus, at some point, you have to go deeper. Freedom comes from having genuine experiences with God through His Word; His Word is the truth that transforms us, a topic we will explore in more depth in the next chapter.

> **WE HAVE AN ACTIVE ROLE IN OUR HEALING. WE PARTICIPATE BY MAINTAINING A RELATIONSHIP WITH GOD AND OBEYING HIS WORD.**

NEWNESS OF LIFE

A physical heart transplant is sometimes necessary to save a person's life. A spiritual heart transplant is always necessary to save us from spiritual death and to enable us to experience both eternal life and the abundant life on earth that Jesus died to give us. You have received a new spiritual heart if you have accepted Jesus Christ as your Lord and Savior—and you enter into the benefits of that new heart and maintain those benefits by staying in close relationship with Him, loving and obeying Him, and allowing Him to heal you of all your hurts. If you have not yet received Christ, I encourage you to enter today into the new life He has provided for you by praying the prayer found at the end of chapter 4.

A new beginning comes with newness of life, restoration, and an open pathway for moving forward. Again, I won't sugarcoat this: the healing process can be painful. Yet it is worth it!

The freedom we enter into through Christ has great purpose. It is intended not only for us to find relief and live in peace and wholeness, but also for us to carry this transformational message to others who are bound. Your "mess" becomes His message of forgiveness, love, grace, and mercy.

You are empowered by the Holy Spirit to help other people be set free through the gospel of Jesus Christ and God's process of change. You are enabled to lead others into an experience of the finished work of Christ on the cross and new life through His resurrection.

Before you move on to the next chapter, stop for a moment. Pause and take a deep breath. Thank God for His great love and mighty work of removing your stony heart and giving you a heart for Him. Know that He is healing you and not harming you. Know that you are worth it and that newness of life awaits you. Say aloud the prayer below, or pray in your own words, to help you meditate on this moment of God's healing power at work within you.

Heavenly Father, I thank You for the mighty work You are doing inside of me. Thank You for my new heart. I completely put my faith and trust in You. In Jesus's name I pray, amen and amen.

I will give you a new heart, and I will put a new spirit in you. I will take out your stony, stubborn heart and give you a tender, responsive heart. (Ezekiel 36:26 NLT)

COURAGE CHOICES FOR YOUR HEALING

1. Are you willing to give God full permission to do His mighty work in you in every area of your life? Tell Him so in your own words, right now. Short, sweet, and to the point will work just fine. Or, take as much time as you need. God is waiting for you. He loves you and desires to heal you, friend. Allow Him to do so.

2. Consider your habits—where you go and what you do every day. Think about what you need to do differently to protect your heart as you heal. Reevaluate your relationships:

   a. Is there anyone with whom you should cut ties?

   b. Which relationships will you keep?

   c. What new hobbies or lifestyle choices will you embrace?

   d. What boundaries must you establish so that God's mighty work is not contaminated during this critical part of your healing process?

3. God's promises are real and true. I challenge you to search the Bible for three Scriptures that encourage you greatly. Write them down on an index card, in the notes on your phone, or in another special way. Then, look at them and read them aloud daily as a reminder of God's greatness, power, faithfulness, and love for you.

8

THE TRUTH THAT TRANSFORMS

There is no greater love than that which comes to us from our Father God through His Son, Jesus Christ. Today, I believe that statement with every fiber of my being. Yet, before trusting Jesus as my Lord and Savior, I had doubts and questions about God's love, and I had uncertainties and fears about following Christ. Sometimes I felt unworthy of God, wondering if I could possibly live a holy life for Him. I often felt that I had fallen too far from grace for Him to accept me. I also questioned how God could be good all the time when there was so much wrong in the world and with my life. The word *believe* is defined as "to have confidence in the truth, the existence, or the reliability of something, although without absolute proof that one is right in doing so."[6] This type of belief in God was hard for me to grasp. I was confused about many things, and I had to dare myself to believe in God's goodness and grace.

As I expressed earlier in this book, I became angry at the Lord for all the negative circumstances in my life. I blamed Him for each heartache I had experienced, for every one of my bad choices, and for my continual struggles with addiction. I assumed that a good and powerful God would fix all my problems and deliver me out of my pain, simply because He could. I wasn't sure what to do with thoughts or feelings that made it difficult for me to trust God. I had never studied the Bible from a position of seeking truth, nor had I ever pursued a personal relationship with Jesus Christ.

---

6. *Dictionary.com*, s.v., "believe," https://www.dictionary.com/browse/believe.

SUCCUMBING TO THE ENEMY'S LIES

Friend, perhaps you're in the same situation I was, or maybe someone close to you is. Our doubts and confusion about God, and/or our anger toward Him, often lead us to stop trusting Him. As a result, we develop erroneous mindsets, make wrong choices, fall into patterns of dysfunctional behavior, and become stuck in a cycle of sin. We believe the enemy's lies about God and ourselves rather than believing God's truth, through which we are transformed by the power of the Holy Spirit and the process of change.

I had a head knowledge of Christ because my parents raised me and my three sisters in the Catholic Church. They took us to mass every Sunday, and they enrolled us in Catholic schools. My loving parents, Gerry and Peggy, made sure that my sisters and I had a foundation of faith in our lives.

The most important commission parents have is raising their children to love God and follow His ways. Parents are to be the initial proof for their offspring that God exists and is almighty, all-powerful, and all-loving. The lives of godly parents are deeply rooted and grounded in Christ and the truth of the Bible. Before their children are born, they pray over them in the womb. And, after their children arrive, they endeavor to make sure their own words, actions, behaviors, and lifestyles line up with the Word of God so they can be vivid illustrations of who God is and how He expects us to live. This way of parenting blesses children with strong spiritual and personal identities. It brings them security as they daily experience genuine, Christlike love.

My parents taught me to love God, but, as I explained in previous chapters, the enemy came to disrupt their mighty work and destroy the purity and power of my identity in Christ through the malicious actions of a neighbor who molested me when I was a child. My fear and confusion started with that violation. At the time, I didn't know this event would change the trajectory of my entire life. It altered my outlook from one of faith and trust to one of fear and frustration. It distorted my vision of who God really is. In response to my pain, I unknowingly erected a barricade around my heart, built with disillusionment and distrust. This created the first roadblock to my belief in the goodness of God and the great value I have in His eyes.

I was too young to understand and process what was happening to me behind closed doors. At Sunday school, we sang the song "Jesus Loves Me":

Jesus loves me, this I know,
For the Bible tells me so.
Little ones to Him belong;
They are weak, but He is strong.

Yes, Jesus loves me.
Yes, Jesus loves me.
Yes, Jesus loves me,
The Bible tells me so.

I couldn't understand how this song could be true when I was being sexually abused. "If Jesus really loves me, why is this happening to me?" I thought. "If Jesus is so strong, why doesn't He rescue me?"

This question haunted me throughout my teenage and young-adult years. I did not know the pathway to healing, so I put this event on the back burner of my mind and heart, not realizing the devastating effects such abuse can have on one's entire life when it is not brought to Father God to be healed. As I grew up, I turned my back on God's love and the truth about Him my parents had taught me and shown me through their life in Him. I walked away from God's great plan for me and the abundant life that awaited me. While my parents had been faithful to raise me in the nurture and admonition of the Lord (see Ephesians 6:4 KJV), my scriptural belief system had been destroyed by the evil that was forced upon me by the wicked actions of another human being.

I now recognize that there are some things we may never have answers for in this life. We may never be able to understand why certain events happened to us or those whom we love. We live in a fallen world where people make bad choices and inflict terrible evil on others. In this world, Satan also seeks to destroy our lives in whatever ways he can.

Yet what I have come to understand about God far outweighs what I still don't understand about the hurtful events of my life. The Bible taught me that both God and the enemy work through people. Every day, each of us decides—knowingly or unknowingly—whose influence we'll follow. God did not inflict sexual abuse or addictions on me, nor did He just sit back and allow them to come into my life. Likewise, God does not afflict you or your loved ones with abuse, addictions, disabilities, or life-threatening diseases. You may be struggling with one or more of these difficulties. Be assured that all afflictions are from the enemy, not from God.

God has given human beings free will to decide whether or not to love, trust, obey, and serve Him. He does not manipulate our free will. If we were "forced" to love God, that would not be genuine love at all. It would not be an expression of our own hearts and wills.

Sadly, I blamed God for the works of the enemy in my life, as well as my own sinful choices. I did not wisely discern between the works of darkness and the works of the Lord. I didn't realize the correlation that, just as the enemy needs a willing vessel to do his bidding, so God needs a surrendered life to work through. Our actions, words, and deeds reveal whether we are trusting in God or in our own devices.

> **GOD HAS GIVEN HUMAN BEINGS FREE WILL TO DECIDE WHETHER OR NOT TO LOVE, TRUST, OBEY, AND SERVE HIM. HE DOES NOT MANIPULATE OUR FREE WILL.**

First Corinthians 14:33 says, "*God is not a God of confusion but of peace*" (ESV). The enemy will try to plant seeds of doubt, distorted thinking, and even anger toward God in your heart as you experience negative life events and situations, with the sole purpose of stealing your faith. He wants you completely separated from God, so he seeks to make it difficult for you to believe in the Lord and to be close to Him. Think about how the hurts of life affect your personal relationships with other people. They undermine intimacy and trust within those relationships. The same result can occur in your relationship with God. Doubt, confusion, and anger can chip away at your faith in God and tempt you to turn away from Him completely.

However, even though the enemy attacks us, sets us up for temptation, and tries to harm us in many ways, God is able to remove the power of our painful memories and expose the lies and distortions we have believed as a result of Satan's deceptions and assaults. The Lord our God is mightier than our adversary, and His truth can penetrate the deepest wounds in our hearts and the greatest hardships of our lives.

REPLACING LIES WITH GOD'S TRUTH

It's important for you to pause and reflect here, friend. Have you ever experienced a life-changing event or received life-altering news that caused you to doubt God or lose your grip on life? Are you aware that stressful circumstances, bad reports, and negative diagnoses can cause roadblocks to your belief in God and derail your life's purpose—or hinder your purpose ever so slowly that you don't realize what is happening until you find yourself frustrated, stuck, and experiencing deep sorrow or defeat? You may even love Jesus deeply at this very moment but still find yourself lost or struggling.

Be encouraged—you are on your way to finding your strength and joy once again! We find renewed strength and joy by rediscovering and embracing the truth about God in Jesus Christ and countering the lies of the enemy. Let's begin to look at what the Bible says regarding God's truth:

- If we follow the teachings of Christ, we will know the truth, and that truth will enable us to live in freedom. *"Jesus said to the people who believed in him, 'You are truly my disciples if you remain faithful to my teachings. And you will know the truth, and the truth will set you free'"* (John 8:31–32 NLT).

- Jesus is the truth. He is the way to heaven, healing, transformation, and so much more. He shows us how to live in a manner that pleases God, reveals the truth that transforms our lives and sets us free, and gives us eternal life. He is both our guide to the Father and the path that leads to Him. *"Jesus told him [Thomas], 'I am the way, the truth, and the life. No one can come to the Father except through me'"* (John 14:6 NLT).

- All of God's Word is living and powerful. It reveals to us our true thoughts and motivations, and it shows us how to align our lives with God's will. *"For the word of God is alive and active. Sharper than any double-edged sword, it penetrates even to dividing soul and* spirit, joints and marrow; it judges the thoughts and attitudes of the heart" (Hebrews 4:12 NIV).

+ The Word of God guides us in every situation and perplexity we face in life. "*Your word is a lamp for my feet, a light on my path*" (Psalm 119:105 NIV).

+ The Word of God leads us perfectly while shielding and protecting us. "*As for God, his way is perfect: the LORD's word is flawless; he shields all who take refuge in him*" (Psalm 18:30 NIV).

+ The Word of God corrects, teaches, prepares, and equips us. "*All Scripture is inspired by God and is useful to teach us what is true and to make us realize what is wrong in our lives. It corrects us when we are wrong and teaches us to do what is right. God uses it to prepare and equip his people to do every good work*" (2 Timothy 3:16–17 NLT).

+ The Word of God restores us and makes us whole. "*The law of the Lord is perfect, restoring the [whole] person; the testimony of the Lord is sure, making wise the simple*" (Psalm 19:7 AMPC).

I could quote many similar passages. From the book of Genesis to the book of Revelation, the Holy Bible is God's love letter to us, revealing His truth for our lives. And all sixty-six books of the Bible point to Christ, showing us how God persistently pursues us with His grace, mercy, and compassion.

It's difficult to express how healing, empowering, and encouraging the truths of the Bible have been for me over the years, especially as I have followed the process of change. I fell in love with this Book, God's manual for our lives, years ago. But the Word is not just a book; Jesus Himself is the Word. (See, for example, John 1:1; 1 John 1:1.) Jesus offers us God's unconditional love, and He powerfully transforms us as we live according to His truth. God is so good, my friend! I came to believe the truth about God by learning that Jesus is my Ally, Savior, and Defender, while the enemy is the perpetrator of evil, harm, and unwarranted afflictions. Because I did not know the truth, I had been blaming God for the enemy's work, the effects of my sinful nature, the poor choices I had made, and the evil choices others made to harm me. I had been blinded to the power of a human being's sinful nature to rule their lives.

JESUS IS OUR ALLY, SAVIOR, AND DEFENDER, WHILE THE ENEMY IS THE PERPETRATOR OF EVIL, HARM, AND UNWARRANTED AFFLICTIONS.

The enemy is cowardly and cunning. He comes to steal, kill, and destroy us when we are too young to fight against him or defend ourselves. He also attacks us when we are older, devising schemes to derail our belief in God through violations, betrayals, and other negative circumstances. Hardships, whether they occur in your life or in the lives of your loved ones, can easily lead you to distrust God if you are not watchful over your heart. The enemy knows that if he can weaken or destroy your faith in Jesus, causing you to question His love, authority, and power, he has gained powerful access to your life. That is what he did to me.

But when we know the truth, it sets us free. In the first part of John 10:10, Jesus was clear about the enemy's plans against us: *"The thief does not come except to steal, and to kill, and to destroy"* (John 10:10 NKJV). Satan comes after us with a vengeance through his evil schemes, lies, and attacks. But in the second portion of this verse, Jesus delivers the great news of His own plan for our lives: *"I have come that they may have life, and that they may have it more abundantly"* (John 10:10 NKJV).

As believers in Christ, when we absorb the Scriptures and grow in our understanding of God's truth, we enter into the abundant life Jesus offers us. We develop godly love and character, reflecting the work of the Holy Spirit who lives in us and works through us. Remember that Galatians 5:22–23 reveals the characteristics of someone whose life is controlled by God's Spirit: *"But the Holy Spirit produces this kind of fruit [evidence] in our lives: love, joy, peace, patience, kindness, goodness, faithfulness, gentleness, and self-control"* (NLT). A person who is not growing in the love of God becomes desensitized to sin's ill effects; they begin to allow another nature to rule and reign within them—the sinful nature.

Such a spirit of darkness lived within the man who repeatedly molested me—and molested many other children for years afterward. When a person chooses to ignore God or rebels against Him, sins of betrayal and violations of the vilest kind can manifest in their life. Before describing the fruit of the Spirit, Galatians 5 explains what results when we allow the sinful nature to control us:

> *When you follow the desires of your sinful nature, the results are very clear: sexual immorality, impurity, lustful pleasures, idolatry, sorcery, hostility, quarreling, jealousy, outbursts of anger, selfish ambition, dissension, division, envy, drunkenness, wild parties, and other sins like these. Let me tell you again, as I have before, that anyone living that sort of life will not inherit the Kingdom of God.*
>
> (Galatians 5:19–21 NLT)

I, too, was enslaved by my own sinful instincts and habits, with seemingly no way of escape, until I learned the truth that would completely set me free: Jesus is my Savior and Lord who delivers me from all evil and heals all my hurts. God is not only a good God, but He is an awesome God! There's no one like Him!

THE ENEMY'S PLAN VERSUS GOD'S PLAN

Below is a chart I developed to help me to better understand the enemy's plan to deceive me and destroy my destiny versus God plan to show me the truth about who I am in Christ and manifest the good purposes He has for me. Sometimes I need the aid of a simple graph like this, where I can see the comparisons side by side, to clearly grasp God's truth and apply it to my life. The Spirit's nature and the sinful nature are constantly at war with one another. But take heart: the nature of the Spirit wins when we submit to God. (See Romans 7; Galatians 5.) The Spirit's nature produces power, faith, hope, and love, while the sinful nature produces darkness, defeat, destruction, and death.

The devil, who seeks to provoke the sinful nature in you, is evil—he is a liar, murderer, and thief, and he seeks to destroy you. In contrast, God is holy, perfect, righteous, and merciful toward you, and His love for you never ends. Through Christ, you have a new life, with everything you need to overcome the devil's schemes and live victoriously. Jesus is fighting for you! Remember, he is your Ally, and not your enemy.

In the following chart, notice how Satan, the enemy—by deceiving us and stirring up our sinful nature—is the problem. Compare this to the way Jesus Christ, the Savior—by offering us His eternal love, power, and truth—is the solution.

THE NATURE OF SATAN, THE ENEMY	THE NATURE OF JESUS, THE SAVIOR
Father of Lies	Author of Truth
Prince of Darkness	Prince of Light and Prince of Peace
Adversary and Accuser	Advocate and Defender
Provokes your sinful nature so you will become powerless and enslaved	Gives you the nature of His Spirit so you will become empowered and free
Defeats and destroys	Adopts and redeems
Condemns, confuses, and corrupts	Comforts, clarifies, changes, and cleanses
Criticizes: "You are pitiful and powerless"	Assures: "You are priceless and powerful"
Accuses: "You are dirty and damaged"	Promises: "You are cleansed and made new"
Lies: "You are worthless and alone"	Speaks the truth: "You are a beloved child of God"
Never forgives or forgets your wrongs	Forgives your sins and remembers them no more
Imposes guilt, shame, and regret on you	Gives you glory, honor, and respect
Promotes hate, lust, and anxiety	Promotes love, hope, and peace
Brings depression and despair	Brings deliverance and direction
Incites frustration, hostility, and harm	Gives you a future, hope, help, and healing
Steals, kills, and destroys	Offers purpose, restoration, and abundant life
Sends forth demons and executes plans of destruction	Sends forth angels and implements plans of success and victory
Inflicts curses, death, hell, and eternal damnation	Bestows blessings, newness of life, heaven, and eternal life

The Bible says that we have all sinned and fallen short of the glory of God. (See Romans 3:23.) Expressions of sin can vary from telling a "little white lie" to committing the vilest of evils. When we live without Jesus, our sins progress over time, and the consequences are danger, delusion, damage, and destruction. But Jesus is the solution to the power, effects, and penalty of our sin; to the wiles of the enemy perpetrated against us; to all of life's hardships; and to each of our hurts that need healing.

A LIFE-CHANGING DECISION

My heart and mind were greatly damaged over the years from the destructive choices I made as I attempted to cope with and mask my broken heart. Again, my misguided choices, and the evil choices of others inflicted against me, caused the trajectory of my life to go severely off course. When I looked for a course correction—for a way back to wholeness—I began to do a self-assessment of the many years in which I had engaged in promiscuity, reckless living, and dysfunctional loving. After that assessment, I had to make a choice to reject the lies of the enemy; admit I was a sinner who needed the one and only Savior, Jesus Christ; and believe wholeheartedly in the Lord. And admit I did!

I stopped turning my back on God and instead performed an exhilarating U-turn, away from my feelings and past experiences as the pathway to formulating my own truth, and toward Jesus as the Truth and the Author and Finisher of my faith. (See Hebrews 12:2.) I did this by abandoning my old ways of thinking and living, and asking Jesus to become my Lord and Savior. I renounced the makeshift beliefs that I had constructed through my own opinions and painful past experiences, and surrendered to the gospel of Jesus Christ. I asked Jesus to save me from the deceitful and delusional power of sin and its deadly bondage. I pledged to devote myself to Him and to learn His ways, trusting that His power would not only save me but also heal, transform, and restore me. In this way, I allowed Jesus, rather than myself or others, to define me, and I allowed the Word of God to transform me. It was a life-changing decision!

The word *gospel* means "good news," and I dared to believe that this good news was true—not just in general, but specifically for me and my life. When I did, God started opening my eyes to His truth and softening my heart toward Him. That's exactly how God operates. Remember, He awaits your permission and invitation to enter or reenter your life. He is a loving God who patiently waits for you to turn to Him. He will not force you to believe in Him.

> **I PERFORMED AN EXHILARATING U-TURN, AWAY FROM MY FEELINGS AND PAST EXPERIENCES AS THE PATHWAY TO FORMULATING MY OWN TRUTH, AND TOWARD JESUS AS THE TRUTH AND THE AUTHOR AND FINISHER OF MY FAITH.**

Frankly, at the start of my journey, I did not have one ounce of desire for God within me. What drew me to Christ was my anger and desperation! I knew there was no other way out for me. I had exhausted all of my own personal, earthly attempts to become healed and whole. As the saying goes, "I was sick and tired of being sick and tired." This passage in Romans best describes my condition at that point in my life:

So the trouble is not with the law, for it is spiritual and good. The trouble is with me, for I am all too human, a slave to sin. I don't really understand myself, for I want to do what is right, but I don't do it. Instead, I do what I hate. But if I know that what I am doing is wrong, this shows that I agree that the law is good. So I am not the one doing wrong; it is sin living in me that does it. And I know that nothing good lives in me, that is, in my sinful nature. I want to do what is right, but I can't. I want to do what is good, but I don't. I don't want to do what is wrong, but I do it anyway. But if I do what I don't want to do, I am not really the one doing wrong; it is sin living in me that does it. I have discovered this principle of life—that when I want to do what is right, I inevitably do what is wrong. I love God's law with all my heart. But there is another power within me that is at war with my mind. This power makes me a slave to the sin that is still within me. Oh, what a miserable person I am! Who will free me from this life that

is dominated by sin and death? Thank God! The answer is in Jesus
Christ our Lord. (Romans 7:14–25 NLT)

With nowhere else to turn, it was time for me to walk by faith and not by sight, and to let God lead me to healing. I have never been the same since, in the best possible way. Jesus's death on the cross was the perfect sacrifice, approved by God for you and for me, to bring about our restoration. God's Word promises that all who believe in Jesus and His finished work on the cross will be saved.

Jesus is the only Savior of any religion who came to earth, died for His people, rose from the dead, and ascended into heaven—and there's undeniable proof that He did all those things. Through faith in Jesus, our sins are forgiven. We are reconciled to God, and we are promised a home in eternity with Him. The power of sin over our lives can now be broken if we follow and obey His Word.

We cannot earn salvation or any of the benefits given to us by God in Christ—we can only receive them by faith. When we accept God's gift of forgiveness and eternal salvation by placing our faith in Jesus's atoning, sacrificial death on the cross and His victorious resurrection from the grave, the Spirit of God is born within us. Consequently, we are now empowered to live for Christ and learn His ways. Jesus will keep His promise to heal the afflictions of our pasts and preserve us in our current hardships. We inherited every benefit and promise of God at the moment of our salvation. And we can spend the rest our lives experiencing what has been freely given to us through God's grace. Healing, restoration, and freedom are blessings of our salvation in Jesus.

I paid a heavy price for rejecting God's truth that transforms and living outside of God's boundaries and standards for so many years. Friend, God established those boundaries and standards to keep us safe, joyous, and free. Moreover, His design for our lives, delivered to us through His Word and His Spirit, is powerful and purposeful. We will explore this topic in the next chapter.

Before you continue, will you give God permission, through faith in the Lord Jesus Christ, to take control of your life and lead you into the truth that transforms? God will not barge in and force you to love Him or surrender to Him. Without your permission, His life-changing power will not be activated. Are you willing to surrender fully to the truth of God's Word, releasing all of your personal roadblocks to belief? If so, I encourage you to say the following prayer out loud:

> Heavenly Father, apart from You, I have nowhere to go in my life. I have come to the end of my own path. I surrender myself fully to You, and I ask You to take control of my life and lead me to Your truth, which will completely transform me from the inside out. I release all the roadblocks to belief in You that I have constructed from the painful experiences of my past and the deceptions of the enemy. Thank You for activating the life-changing power of Your Spirit in my life even now, and for giving me the courage to heal. In Jesus's name, amen.

COURAGE CHOICES FOR YOUR HEALING

1. Revisit the questions at the beginning of the section "Replacing Lies with God's Truth." What life-changing events, life-altering news, stressful circumstances, bad reports, or negative diagnoses may have caused you to doubt God's love for you and/or led you to distrust Him? Write down what immediately comes to mind.

2. How did your response to the above situations affect you and the pursuit of your life's purpose? After reading this chapter, do you now see these events in a different light? If so, in what way? In the future, how can you choose a different response when you encounter life's difficulties?

3. List several lies of the enemy you have frequently succumbed to over the years. In what areas of your life do you seem to be most vulnerable to Satan's deceptions and attacks? List three Scriptures that counteract these lies with God's transforming truth.

4. To better discern and reject the work of Satan in your life, review the chart in this chapter, making note of the clear differences between the nature of Satan, the enemy, and the nature of Jesus Christ, the Savior. Which of these distinctions seemed to speak to you the most? Which opened your eyes to an area in which you may have been deceived? Which taught you the most about God's love for you?

5. Have you made the life-changing decision to give God permission, through faith in the Lord Jesus Christ, to take control of your life and lead you into the truth that transforms? You don't have to wait until you come to the very end of yourself, as I did. I encourage

you to give God permission to direct your life from now on so you can discover His great power to heal and restore you! As the starting point of your new life, make a record of your decision to place your faith in Christ. Then, refer to your decision whenever you are tempted to go back to your old lifestyle. Reach out to a strong, loving Christian or group of Christians who can support you in your life-changing decision.

9

PERSEVERANCE, PURPOSE, AND THE POWER OF THE SPIRIT

So long, familiar lifestyle of defeat—I'm forging forward!"

I love that statement because it is empowering. It is a declaration that we have made a courage choice not to stay mired in destructive patterns, addictions, and other life-controlling issues but to move forward in faith according to our new life in Christ.

One of my favorite books of the Bible is the book of Ruth. It contains four chapters of encouragement and inexplicable (from a human standpoint) victories that highlight the importance of persevering in order to endure trying times and fulfill God's purposes. This Old Testament story provides the historical account of how one woman's choices to pursue God's plan for her life in the midst of a distressing situation transformed her hopelessness and despair into a legacy of faith that can be traced to the lineage of Christ Himself.

Ruth was a young, barren widow from the pagan land of Moab. She accompanied Naomi, her elderly mother-in-law, who had also been widowed, on a perilous trek across rugged, mountainous terrain to Naomi's homeland of Judah. With love and concern, Naomi repeatedly told Ruth to take the safe route back to her family, where she could find security with a new husband. But Ruth remained faithful to her commitment to God, to her mother-in-law, and to God's plan for her life. She promised Naomi, *"Wherever you go, I will go; wherever you live, I will live. Your people will be my people, and your God will be my God. Wherever you die, I will die, and there I will be buried. May the* LORD *punish me severely if I allow anything but death to separate us!"* (Ruth 1:16–17 NLT).

Even more important than Ruth's loyalty to Naomi was her unyielding commitment to the Lord and perseverance in following His plan for her life. Will you do the same, friend? Will you commit yourself wholehearted to the Lord and persevere in His purpose for your own life? God has turned my dysfunctions and tragedies into a godly legacy, one that my children can now respect, honor, and be proud of. He has enabled my life to become an example of His faithfulness that can live on from generation to generation. It is an example that He is using even now to snatch lost and broken souls out of the enemy's hands and bring them back to life. Oh, what a mighty God we serve!

"YOU HAVE TO GO THROUGH TO GET TO"

Friend, there will be many times in your life when you will need to "fight the good fight" through persevering faith. (See 1 Timothy 6:12.) My surrender to Jesus and the truths of His Word initiated my transformation, but it took perseverance for a complete transformation to occur. Following Christ and His ways is where freedom lies, yet remaining steady in your choice to follow Him will challenge every fiber of your being at times. You will be pulled out of your comfort zone and into the arena of courage. Make no mistake about it: obeying God includes forsaking the familiar and journeying into the unknown. But you can also be assured of this: when you walk with God by faith, instead of walking according to what you think is right and best, you can trust in the Faithful One who holds your future. Your future in God will be far better than what you could ever imagine your future might hold. Abandoning your old, familiar ways of living, and instead embracing God-directed change, is a sure remedy for success. Ruth's story reminds us that, even in our darkest hour, in times of great loss and suffering, God has a plan to lead us through to safety and deliverance if we will—allow me say it again and again—*trust and obey Him.*

I like to quote the saying "You have to go through to get to." When you are not instantly "evacuated" out of a problem, you must persevere through it. I have learned that trusting God and following His exit strategy, rather than my own, comes with His protection and provision. In this faith journey, God leads me every step of the way. In the past, when I tried to overcome my problems by myself, all I did was run from one problem to the next. Yes, God's path to freedom can be painful, and it takes time, but as I have been emphasizing throughout this book, it's worth it. *You* are worth it! Please remember that. Keep moving in God's direction, one step at a time, one day at a time, and one choice at a time, and you will receive your healing and freedom.

OUR GOOD SHEPHERD SUSTAINS US IN THE JOURNEY

As you "go through to get to," you will experience situations and circumstances that require much patience and endurance. I know that many of those situations will also require tough courage choices. The key is to trust God as you experience the pain of the trial, understanding that He is your Protector, and He has a divine plan to move you past the place of despair, stagnancy, hopelessness, or sorrow in which you find yourself. While faith in God can seem risky and, at times, counterintuitive, His purposes never fail, and they are always exponentially better than our own.

When we choose God's way out of our pain, we will come to know Him as the Good Shepherd that King David described in Psalm 23. A shepherd's job is to protect their sheep from harm and guide them to green pastures for grazing and rest, and fresh streams to quench their thirst. They lead their sheep along paths that will enable them to flourish, and they redirect them from wandering away from the safety of the fold lest they fall to their destruction. Shepherds care for the health and safety of their sheep like loving parents care for the well-being of their children.

When you allow Jesus to shepherd your life, He supernaturally fulfills your heartfelt longings for validation, acceptance, love, peace, joy, and happiness. With His rod, He protects you, and with His staff, He guides you. The Good Shepherd will never leave you or betray your trust.

RESISTING THE OLD, FAMILIAR PATTERNS

On this healing journey, you will face the temptation to quit the fight of faith and go back to those old, familiar patterns of dysfunctional loving and living. To this day, it baffles me how our minds can trick us into thinking that returning to the familiar—no matter how unsatisfactory or painful—is somehow safer than venturing into the unknown, amazing future God promises us. It is as if we think defeat will have some grand payout.

Instead, we must stay the course. I have learned that our journey to healing and restoration has both a purpose and an expiration date. The pain of change is worth it because, with every passing day, we experience more and more healing, and the pain becomes less and less. In contrast, the pain of staying in the same condition might lie dormant for a season, but it always resurfaces with a vengeance, stealing more precious time from you that could be used toward fulfilling your destiny.

The temptation to fall back into the familiar is an embedded, learned behavior that your survival-mode instincts have come to rely on. Previously, you had nothing to offer in place of that default behavior. But that is no longer true! Through the power of God and the process of change, you have learned the way of escape from defeat, and you know how to live as the new healthy and whole you. You now have positive steps to take and healthy choices to make!

IN OUR JOURNEY TO HEALING AND RESTORATION, PAIN HAS BOTH A PURPOSE AND AN EXPIRATION DATE.

AT A CROSSROADS

As I described in chapter 1, the day I put my boys on an airplane with one-way tickets to go live with my ex-husband after signing over my parental custody rights, I was faced with a severe temptation to quit my journey to healing. The drive home from the airport felt like the lowest point of my entire life. I experienced a sense of devastation that I could never adequately convey in words. But because I had recently put my faith in Jesus Christ, my utter despair and gut-wrenching pain came with an acute awareness of God's abiding presence. I now had something powerful within me to offer the dark voice of despair that tempted me to give up and accept defeat.

I had a life-changing, courage choice to make amid my great pain and hopelessness. My mind was telling me there was no longer a reason to move forward or even live for another day. I thought I had lost my very reason for living. It seemed as if my new life in Christ had all been in vain, offering no real benefits—as if the promises of victory in Christ I had been holding on to were all a sham. I wanted to bolt, return to my former lifestyle, and rekindle my anger toward God. If you've been in the same dark place—if you are there right now—I think you know exactly what I mean.

I was at a crossroads. My emotional reserves were empty, I felt no spark of hope, and there was no one and nothing on earth that could take away my intense despair and heartbreak or make things better in any way, shape, or form. The desire to relapse was almost overwhelming. Thoughts of destruction were pulsating in my mind, consuming my very being. Naturally speaking, there was nothing inside me that wanted to stay on the right path. I wanted to numb every part of me and escape from a reality that seemed impossible to bear.

And yet, in the midst of this crushing pain, even though I was broken and bitter, I *chose* to drive straight home. Instead of escaping to a drug house, party scene, or lustful encounter, I cried out to God in my SUV, sobbing and mourning the forfeiture of my parental rights while still declaring, "God, I choose You." I made the right choice by deciding to embrace my new life in Christ instead of throwing my life away. I made a courage choice: I chose to let victory win, even though that victory wouldn't be instantaneous. I put my trust in God and His process of change, and I activated my new successful ways of dealing with life. Instead of making a dark decision that would lead to more defeat, I sought help through my mentor, Laura, and found shelter in her safety and love.

When I made the right choices and continually persevered, I won! Each day, as I made more positive choices through the power of God and the new life principles I had learned, I actively experienced victory in the middle of seeming defeat. Don't miss what I just said: loss and victory were competing with one another, but I consistently chose victory. Because of the choices I made more than twenty years ago, I moved into a position of faith, power, and strength. I was able to make the courage choice to persevere because I had my plan of success and victory already in place, and I put it into action. That plan included actively planting the Word of God in my heart by reading and studying the Bible, setting aside time for prayer each day, being involved in a local body of believers, and establishing a support system (including having godly mentors and friends on speed dial). As we persevere in our healing, it is essential that we regularly receive spiritual and emotional support. (To this day, I call twenty-four-hour prayer lines whenever I am in need of prayer and encouragement, if the people in my regular support system are not available.)

YOUR OWN VICTORY PLAN

Friend, I was able to stay the course during the darkest period of my life, and you can too. Throughout your lifetime, until Jesus returns to earth or calls you to heaven, you will be faced with similar choices to persevere. Whether things are good, bad, or somewhere in between, you will always have the option to choose power over weakness, freedom over defeat, and right over wrong.

Do you have a victory plan in place? Prepare that plan now so you can draw on it every day and rely on it when you especially need it. That plan should include regularly sowing the Word of God in your heart and mind by Bible reading, study, and memorization. Then, when you are faced with the temptation to quit, God's Word will rise up within you like a mighty force, keeping you from evil and self-destruction. When you need the power of the Scriptures to overcome whatever you are facing, the Holy Spirit will release exactly the right words into your spirit. When your mind and emotions want to give up, if you choose to worship God, obey His Word, call a godly friend for support, and continue to walk in the path of righteousness, you will experience God's power and victory over Satan's attacks.

You will win the battle if you keep obeying God. Obeying simply means to choose what's right, one choice at a time. The Spirit of God within you will show you the way to safety, convicting you when you are headed into danger and diverting you from harm. God is faithful all the time and will show up in every difficult situation of your life if you refuse to be knocked off-center by a rush of feelings designed by the enemy to lead you into defeat and destruction. I'm referring to exercising real faith over your fear and despair—not just repeating nice-sounding Christian slogans about faith. Speaking Word-based expressions of your trust and reliance on God has great power! This power will enable you to course-correct and equip you to withstand the storm. Spiritual power that comes from speaking God's Word by His Spirit is a force to be reckoned with. It will conquer every demon in hell and cast down every assignment the enemy has devised against you. This is what it means to have persevering faith by which you can forge forward and wave the victory flag.

Don't you dare quit! Remember, you have to go through the process of healing and restoration to experience victory on the other side. Keep fighting the good fight of faith. The right choice is always the right choice. God's plan is simple: daily walking by faith. It's our unruly emotions and desires that are difficult. They create stumbling blocks that threaten to knock us out of the ring of faith. Choosing to follow the familiar, past ways of defeat and dysfunction is never the right decision. Darkness will never produce light. Going back will never produce victory. But following God's light and persevering in Christ will win the battle and conquer the darkness every time.

The positive results I gained from making right choices are more powerful than the bad results I experienced from making wrong choices. My broken heart has been fully restored. What if I had quit? Turned back to darkness? Made the wrong choice by giving in to the unbearable pain, imagining I was imprisoned by circumstances that seemed to offer no way out? Ask yourself the same question right now, friend: what if you were to quit, choosing to stay stuck in dysfunction and pain, and failing to move forward? Play out that scenario all the way, with great honesty and truth. What would your life be like?

Had I chosen to believe Satan's lie, as Eve did in the garden of Eden, taking his cunning bait, my heart would not have been healed, I would not enjoy a strong marriage today, and I would not be reconciled to my sons. But through my abiding faith in Christ, the support of my Christian friends, prayer, and continued right living, I persevered, and the reward was infinitely worth the journey!

> **KEEP FIGHTING THE GOOD FIGHT OF FAITH.**
> **THE RIGHT CHOICE IS ALWAYS THE RIGHT CHOICE.**

LET HEALING TAKE THE TIME IT NEEDS

Persevering faith is needed because healing and restoration are a process. In situations that have produced unbearable pain and consequences, healing takes time. I had to trust the process, which, in my case, lasted for years, not just days, weeks, or months. The process was tough and painful. But, during those years, I experienced many daily victories. I wouldn't trade my life in Christ for anything or anyone! I have learned to trust God in all things. I have learned to love and serve the Lord through times of struggle when life didn't seem to make sense and God appeared to be absent. I have learned to trust His process throughout many years of believing, waiting, and obeying Him.

Lately, on social media, I've noticed many people promoting the idea that God promises a "suddenly," an "instant miracle," or a "twenty-four-hour turnaround" if you will just do one simple thing or answer the call for a donation in that moment. Be careful of such bait-and-switch messages that prey on your desperation. If you give a donation because the Holy Spirit has led you to do so, then that is a righteous action. But if you keep giving donations out of your anxiety, fear, or pain, hoping it will convince God to instantly deliver you from the healing and restoration process, then you are setting yourself up for a faith failure. The restoration process takes time, and you will be tested in the midst of it.

Let me be clear: sometimes, God does immediately come to our rescue when we have a particular need or are in danger. The Bible gives us examples of this, and many believers since biblical times have experienced the same. However, life is not filled with "suddenlies" from God that will rescue us from the process of change. The process is where we become healed, restored, and transformed. God help me if He *had* answered my cries to have my children back "suddenly." They would have returned to the same mother with the same bad character that had rendered me powerless to raise them correctly. My children needed the godly mother I was always created to be and was fighting to become. They deserved that, and so did I.

When I first became clean and sober, I still had a craving for drugs and alcohol but persevered by listening to godly direction and putting it into action. Then, one day, after struggling for so long, I was set free, and I realized the craving was gone.

I trusted and obeyed God, embracing His sustaining power, for ten years. *Then* the opportunity for one of my sons to come back and live with me was presented. Within five more years, I would be fully restored to the other two boys as well.

You will experience victory, too, on the other side of patience, endurance, and perseverance. Again, this will require that you do not quit, no matter what. Do not choose to live life in reverse but rather continually move forward in faith. Keep progressing in God's power, direction, strength, and leading. Keep obeying. Choose the godly path every time instead of some of the time. As you totally put your trust in God, you will have to fight to experience the miraculous outcome you seek. It will not be easy. It's not going to be a "twenty-four-hour turnaround." But it will produce within you a persevering faith that will allow you to get through anything you will ever face in life.

God doesn't always answer my prayers the way I want them to be answered, but I have come to trust that His plans are greater than mine, and they are always for my good, even when I can't see it at the time. I know from experience that God is faithful, and He will give me what I need even when I can't comprehend why I need it. There are many life situations that I do not understand. Why did things happen as they did? I've stopped torturing myself trying to figure it all out. Again, there are just some things we will never have answers to or be able to fathom. If we're intellectually honest, we will admit that if we could understand everything about God and why He does certain things or allows various things to happen, then

He wouldn't be God, and our faith would be in vain. The Bible says that His ways are higher than our ways, and His thoughts are unfathomable to the mere human mind. (See Isaiah 55:8–9.)

Because of God's power and my devotion to Him, He delivered me from every destructive desire and brought me out of every dark, emotional season. He has always kept my feet on solid ground. I want you to learn how to persevere in the same way. You first need to acknowledge that things are not always going to turn out the way you planned; however, through and in Christ, all things are possible. (See, for example, Matthew 19:26.) I can testify from the depths of my soul that the ultimate victory is worth it. The Holy Spirit will keep you from being crushed or defeated if you listen to His guidance and follow the path on which He leads you. His power will enable you to overcome. We will talk more about the power of the Holy Spirit later in this chapter. Beyond a shadow of a doubt, I know that God is good all the time. I know that He is the Restorer. I know that He is the Waymaker, and so much more.

God's Word reveals that His character and heart are unchanging. As you come to understand this truth, it will increase your faith capacity and give you the ability to stand strong in the midst of the hard times. God works His will and good pleasure today in the same way He always has. He judges sin, and yet He is forgiving, merciful, and patient. Across the ages, ever since Adam and Eve's sinful choice in the garden of Eden marred God's perfect creation, God has been on a rescue mission to save people from condemnation and to set them free from the bondage of sin's grip on their lives. He rescues them from behind enemy lines. He still sets free those who are enslaved to sin when they trust in Jesus as the Way, the Truth, and the Life. (See John 14:6.)

As I wrote earlier, the daily choices we make determine the course of our lives and the nature of our healing journey. Our choices set us up for success or failure, healing or heartache, peace or torment, life or death. These choices will position us to experience God's favor and blessing or enslave us to a cycle of sin and dysfunction. And the choices we make often have an effect on our family members, friends, neighbors, coworkers, and others. Consequently, we are not immune to the consequences of our choices or others' decisions. But, remember, we serve a God who gives us a fresh start and a new life.

DO NOT CHOOSE TO LIVE LIFE IN REVERSE BUT RATHER CONTINUALLY MOVE FORWARD IN FAITH. KEEP PROGRESSING IN GOD'S POWER, DIRECTION, STRENGTH, AND LEADING.

CREATED ON PURPOSE, FOR A PURPOSE

By persevering, not only do we receive healing, but we are also enabled to move forward in the purposes God has for our lives. In my life, one courage choice after another led me to a profound experiential understanding that I was fearfully and wonderfully made by God and that I was made *on* purpose, *for* a purpose.

Let Psalm 139:13–16 begin to reveal these awesome truths to you as well:

For you formed my inward parts; you knitted me together in my mother's womb. I praise you, for I am fearfully and wonderfully made. Wonderful are your works; my soul knows it very well. My frame was not hidden from you, when I was being made in secret, intricately woven in the depths of the earth. Your eyes saw my unformed substance; in your book were written, every one of them, the days that were formed for me, when as yet there was none of them. (ESV)

There is nothing in me or about me of which God is not aware. He knows my greatest strengths and all my shortcomings. He has observed all the good I've ever done and all the wrongs I've ever committed. You and I are no surprise to God. He created us spiritually before we were ever physically born into this world. And God created us with a purpose. He gave us natural gifts and talents as well as spiritual gifts so we can be about His business and forge forward in our destinies. A little later, I will talk more about spiritual gifts.

Romans 11:29 delivers this powerful news: *"For God's gifts and his call can never be withdrawn"* (NLT). There is nothing that can disqualify us from the gifts and talents God has given us for the purposes He planned since before the beginning of time. Friend, His gifts are irrevocable. That means your gifts were never lost, no matter what road you have taken up to now. His gifts are still inside of you, just waiting for you to discover and develop them.

Thus, regardless of your past or present circumstances, God has a call on your life, and He has given you gifts and talents to carry it out. Additionally, He will take what the enemy meant for evil against you and use it for your good. (See Genesis 50:20.) God causes all things to come together for the good of those who love Him and are called according to His purpose. (See Romans 8:28.) This promise is for every son and daughter of God—not just for some of them, but *all* of them. That includes you, friend. And here's even greater news: God is the one who empowers you for it all and through it all. You are called. You have gifts. And the Bible says that God Himself equips those whom He calls. (See, for example, Hebrews 13:20–21.) None of us is qualified to serve God by our own merits. But we can persevere right into our God-given purposes through the power of the Holy Spirit.

LIVING IN THE POWER OF THE SPIRIT

When you fully surrender your life to doing God's will, you will become hungry for the power and purpose He has given you. Throughout this book, I have talked about how I relied on the power of the Holy Spirit to receive my healing and remain faithful to God—from the day of that early prayer meeting where I received God's peace and deliverance from Satan's oppression, to the supernatural strength I experienced the day I wanted to give up after losing custody of my boys, to the courage I was given when I had to take a stand for my marriage and not lose myself in the process. As I increasingly yielded myself to the Holy Spirit's life-changing power, protection, and provision, I was transformed, strengthened, and molded for God's purpose for my life.

Likewise, it is the Holy Spirit who will enable you to persevere, live out every part of your life in Christ, and fulfill your God-given purpose. You cannot live a life of faith without relying on the work of the Holy Spirit in and through you. I cannot stress enough the importance of yielding to the Spirit and being baptized in His power in order to stand strong and fulfill God's will.

The Holy Spirit is the very essence of God who comes to live inside of you the moment you are spiritually born again. Shortly after I publicly professed my faith in Jesus for the forgiveness of my sins to receive the promise of eternal life, I was water baptized at the church I attended. Water baptism is a symbolic expression of the Christian faith through which believers personally identify with, and publicly testify to, the death, burial, and resurrection of Jesus Christ. When a new Christian is submerged in water for baptism, it's a picture of how they have died to their old way of life apart from God and been raised to new life in Christ. I will forever cherish my memories of being baptized alongside my sons before they went to live with their father. After I came to faith in Christ, I poured my life into my children while teaching them God's Word. They witnessed the radical change in my life and the unbounding joy of my salvation, and they subsequently professed their faith in Jesus as well. My sons saw firsthand the transforming power of the Spirit in my life.

Similarly, when you received the Holy Spirit, you experienced new life in Christ, and you became filled with God's abiding presence. The word *baptize* comes from the Greek term *baptizo*, which means to be immersed or submerged. I love this meaning. Picture in your mind being completely immersed in God as every aspect of your life is saturated with His divine attributes. His great love for you; His character, which is being formed in you; His forgiveness; and His healing power all flow through you like rivers of living water. This is what His Spirit does!

Attempting to heal, forgive, move forward in life, find purpose and power, and become everything God has created you to be without the help of the Holy Spirit is impossible. "'*Not by might nor by power, but by my Spirit,' says the LORD Almighty*" (Zechariah 4:6 NIV). God is your Creator, and it is His power, and His power alone, that saves, transforms, heals, and restores you; it is His power that defines your purpose and equips your call. His supernatural power is able to bring you through all circumstances and achieve anything He leads you to do. When you have received the Holy Spirit, healing is alive inside of you!

God gives us everything we need to resist Satan's temptations and reject his counterfeit truths through the power and wisdom of the Holy Spirit, who teaches and guides us. Before ascending to heaven after His resurrection from the grave, Jesus told His disciples that He had to leave so the Holy Spirit could come to continually live inside of them: *"But very truly I tell you, it is for your good that I am going away. Unless I go away, the Advocate will not come to you; but if I go, I will send him to you"* (John 16:7 NIV). The Holy Spirit is the ultimate Comforter, all-wise counsel, and supernatural power of God.

The word *power* refers to the ability to get results. When I was stuck in dysfunction and addiction, I needed results, friend, results that were beyond my own ability to accomplish. Not just from the perspective of attaining freedom and transformation, but also from the standpoint of being able to fulfill my purpose. I wanted to live a life of both power and purpose. Jesus said, *"But you will receive power when the Holy Spirit comes upon you. And you will be my witnesses, telling people about me everywhere— in Jerusalem, throughout Judea, in Samaria, and to the ends of the earth"* (Acts 1:8 NLT).

There is nothing like the power, peace, and joy the Holy Spirit brings. When God's Spirit comes upon you, you will never be the same. Although we receive the Holy Spirit at salvation, we also need to be continually filled with the Spirit and touched by Him. We need to be baptized anew by the Holy Spirit to serve the purposes of our callings. (See, for example, John 20:22; Acts 2:1–4; 4:31; Ephesians 5:18.) Each day, ask God to fill you afresh with the power of His Spirit. We all need a touch from God, a move of His Spirit. It's what the church needs. It's what the world needs.

The Holy Spirit can permeate the deep places of your heart that no human being can reach, not even the greatest Christian counselor, psychiatrist, doctor, or treatment center. I am not at all against using any of those types of assistance. In fact, I encourage you to use such services. They are God-given resources to help you along the way. But what I am saying is that, without the power of the Holy Spirit, your efforts to change and to serve God will ultimately be in vain. You experience the power of God deep within you through His abiding presence. God is Spirit, and He connects to us, with us, and through us by His Spirit: *"For God is Spirit, so those who worship him must worship in spirit and in truth"* (John 4:24 NLT).

Oh, that we would seek the Lord with all our hearts and trust in Him with all our might, worshipping Him in Spirit and in truth. Oh, that we would become fully reliant on God through the power of His Holy Spirit. If we would continually immerse ourselves in the Spirit, allowing Him to control our lives, then we would become healed and whole, a people with great power, carrying out the purposes of God in this world. No evil force, person, or situation would hold us back or shut us down. No betrayal, violation, or feeling of guilt or shame would ever stop us again! Our hearts would be healed, our minds would be sound, and our souls would be on fire for God. We would be unstoppable!

> **IT IS GOD'S POWER, AND HIS POWER ALONE, THAT SAVES, TRANSFORMS, HEALS, AND RESTORES YOU; IT IS HIS POWER THAT DEFINES YOUR PURPOSE AND EQUIPS YOUR CALL.**

SERVING OTHERS THROUGH THE SPIRIT'S GIFTS

The Holy Spirit fills us with His supernatural power not only to heal us, but also to enable us to serve others for God's glory. One of the ways He does this is by giving us spiritual gifts. In 1 Corinthians 12, the apostle Paul wrote:

There are different kinds of spiritual gifts, but the same Spirit is the source of them all. There are different kinds of service, but we serve the same Lord. God works in different ways, but it is the same God who does the work in all of us. A spiritual gift is given to each of us so we can help each other. (1 Corinthians 12:4–7 NLT)

When I became a Christian, I didn't know the diamond in the rough that I truly was in Christ. One of the first evidences of my new life in the Spirit was that I had an insatiable hunger and thirst for the Word of God. This seemed especially unusual for me because I had been an apathetic student throughout high school. I hated studying, and I struggled with academics in general—so much so that I failed the English and writing entrance exam for community college. Yet, today, through the power of the

Spirit, I am an author of books and curriculum with an earned doctorate in biblical studies who teaches God's Word around the world. How did I accomplish this? The Holy Spirit endowed me with the spiritual gift of teaching. But before I could teach others how to apply a biblical worldview to their lives by obeying the inerrant and infallible Word of God, I had to become a dedicated and disciplined student of the Bible. Whether or not you have the spiritual gift of teaching God's Word, studying the Bible is essential for knowing and doing God's will for your life. Faithfully studying the Bible will also help you to discover and use your particular spiritual gifts for the good of others and for God's glory.

In the early days of my recovery, never in a million years would I have imagined that God would use a woman with a past like mine, or commission me to share my testimony of healing and deliverance as my lifelong purpose. But, over time, the blessings, call, and gifts of God became evident in my life. All that He purposed for me started to become my reality. He turned my "mess" into His message of hope and redemption. He completely restored me. And out of my sorrows have come indescribable joy and fulfillment. God has called me to crisis ministry, to help those who are broken and lost in some of the worst ways—to love them, lead them, and guide them into His great love and transforming power.

Likewise, fulfilling your God-given destiny through the gifts and talents He's given you will always, in some way, involve helping others who are going through the same struggles God has delivered you from and continually empowers you to overcome. Some struggles may seem to last a lifetime, but God gives us His power to overcome all things through Him, along with the people and resources we need to thrive. Keep believing! Keep pursuing Jesus!

God redeems every single of one of our trials for our good and for His glory. Someone is waiting on the other side of our obedience. What if I hadn't written this book for you to read? The process of writing it has been excruciating work for me, but it has also been worth every word and moment of my time. Why? Because *you're* worth it! Because God uses people to help people. He always has, and He always will. I wouldn't be here today without the faithful servants of God who answered His call on their lives. You wouldn't be here, either, without the help of others. None of us would be.

To whom is God calling you to deliver hope and help today? Again, He will often use the testimony of your trials and victories to encourage and sustain others. God will reveal your purpose, place, and position in Him as you seek Him and then faithfully prepare to answer His call. Fulfilling your call may not be easy. Everything worthwhile comes with challenges and a price to pay, but you will receive great reward in the end.

My friend, there is nothing more rewarding than to see lives won back to Christ, people set free, and families restored. God calls some believers to give money to organizations that spread the message of God's hope and help while meeting people's tangible needs. Other believers are called to teach, preach, disciple, and do other works of ministry. Many people are called to hospitality, bringing refreshment to the spirits and souls of others. We can show the love and joy of Christ in a variety of ways as we serve other people. For example, we can use our gifts of crafting, knitting or crocheting, cooking, accounting, construction, restoring old cars, playing sports with others—just doing life together, friend! It's not just about preaching from the pulpit or leading a Bible study. The truth, power, and love of God have to be demonstrated as practical and real to people through our lives. We are God's heart, hands, and feet in this world.

In my calling, I travel around the world teaching and preaching, and I use print and electronic materials in various forms to disciple and strengthen others. Additionally, Darryl and I welcome precious souls to come and stay at our house so they can become spiritually and emotionally healed by being loved and led into truth. I also make meals for people, and my husband and I entertain in our home through get-togethers that include barbecues, games, and other fun events. We invite people into our home who have nowhere to go for holidays or no family members who can celebrate with them and love them. Many people have experienced the severe pain of loss and burned bridges in their lives. We allow God to use us to fill that void and help heal the hearts of the sick, suffering, and lost.

Remember, God created us on purpose and for His purposes in this world. The Lord does not show favoritism regarding who receives salvation, His wonder-working power, and His calls. This means that His promises and gifting are available for all who will seek and receive Him. That includes you.

Commit to living God's way. Do not be scared of the healing process. God is with you, and He is for you. He wants to help you have a new start in life. Jesus meant what He said in Matthew 6:33: *"But seek first the kingdom of God and his righteousness, and all these things will be added to you"* (ESV). Get excited, friend! Persevere into your purpose through the power of the Holy Spirit, and experience more joy and fulfillment than you've ever known before. You are worth it!

COURAGE CHOICES FOR YOUR HEALING

1. Put a concrete plan in place that will enable you to be victorious as you persevere in your healing. The elements of your plan should include details regarding a program for reading and studying the Bible; having a regular time each day for worship, prayer, and seeking God; establishing a support system of Christian friends and mentors you can reach out to regularly and when you are in crisis; being active in a local church fellowship where you can serve and receive discipleship training; and participating in a Christian recovery or support group if you struggle with addiction or have suffered emotional and/or physical trauma. Write out your plan, and make sure it is very specific so you will be able to follow it clearly. Commit to putting your plan into practice every day.

2. What natural gifts and talents has God given you? How have you seen God use them in your life? Which spiritual gifts have you received since your salvation? How is God calling you to serve others through them? Pay attention to all these gifts in your life and seek to develop them as God leads.

3. How much do you currently rely on the Holy Spirit to protect, lead, and guide you in life? Friend, study what the Bible teaches and reveals about the Holy Spirit! Each day, ask the Spirit to fill you with God's power so you can persevere in faith in the midst of all types of life circumstances, understand and follow your purpose in life, and reach out to others with the love and grace of the heavenly Father.

10

OPEN DOORS AND ENDLESS POSSIBILITIES: THE NEW YOU!

You are an overcomer, friend! I wrote this book so you could know the same love of God, the same healing, and the same spiritual power that transformed my life. You do not have to live in defeat or remain hopeless. Your past does not define you. God's power within you will change you as you make one courage choice at a time.

Jesus declared, "*I am the vine; you are the branches. Those who remain in me, and I in them, will produce much fruit. For apart from me you can do nothing*" (John 15:5 NLT). My life is Exhibit A of this faithful promise from Jesus. When I started running *to* God instead of *away* from Him, He redeemed every hardship in my life for my good and His glory. As I wrote in the previous chapter, God has transformed what was once a tragedy into a legacy of His faithfulness for me, for my family, and for many others.

The girl who barely graduated from high school now holds a doctoral degree in biblical studies. The former waitress, telemarketer, personal trainer, and real estate agent now teaches God's Word to thousands of people around the world every year and is the owner of multiple successful businesses. Whereas I was once facing a mountain of financial debt and living with my parents as an adult, God has turned my financial devastation into prosperity and generosity. And my marriage and family relationships, which were once in shambles, have been completely restored and are flourishing.

I've been on this amazing transformational journey for over two decades, and I'm not stopping now! God still has more for me, and I'm going after it all through my pursuit of Him. I'm going to continue to love and live without limits because I'm now free to do so.

In *The Courage to Heal*, you have learned the story of how Christ set me free, and He will do the same for you, friend. What victories, open doors, dreams, goals, and possibilities await you? There is an abundant life on the other side of healing! Your former destructive habits, as well as your past and your pain, do not define you, nor are they your destiny to embrace. God doesn't merely bandage us up so we can survive. He completely transforms us so we can thrive through His great power and love.

As you continue to follow the ways of Jesus, He will perform a miraculous work within you and through you. The Bible uses the word "walk" to describe our movement through life, including the lens through which we look at ourselves, our circumstances, and the world; the choices we make along the way; and the character with which we operate. (See, for example, Romans 6:4; Galatians 5:16.) Your perspective on life will drastically change as you move forward into healing and wholeness. Even now, you have gained true spiritual understanding and are beginning to participate in the process of change that will lead to powerful and amazing results!

When you walked in your own will and ways, tainted and influenced by the sinful nature, you lived in agreement with the enemy's plan to steal, kill, and destroy you. No more! You are now ready to walk out the truths you have learned for the rest of your life. Open doors that no human being can shut stand before you. New opportunities wait to be embraced. Your dreams are about to become your reality. Your goals are on the threshold of being achieved. Your victory is ready to be won. Go for it, friend!

At the same time, remember that you must continue in the love of God and the power of the Spirit to keep from falling back into your old ways. We never grow out of the foundational truths that set us free—we grow *from* them. We must never forget them or stop putting them into practice. Once we are set free, we remain free through our daily walk with Christ.

WHAT VICTORIES, OPEN DOORS, DREAMS, GOALS, AND POSSIBILITIES AWAIT YOU? THERE IS AN ABUNDANT LIFE ON THE OTHER SIDE OF HEALING!

FIVE FOUNDATIONAL PRINCIPLES

So, how do we follow God's command to *"walk by the Spirit, and…not gratify the desires of the flesh"* (Galatians 5:16 NIV)? Here are five foundational principles, highlighted from our discussions throughout this book, that will keep you aligned with God's promises and purpose for your life:

1. Study God's Word.

2. Pray: speak *and* listen.

3. Spend time with fellow believers.

4. Safeguard your life.

5. Proceed with caution.

1. STUDY GOD'S WORD

The Bible is the instruction manual for our lives. The words of Scripture are inspired by God's Spirit. They are His written communications to us. If you obey the Bible's instructions and commands, you will remain delivered, healed, and whole. The number one way God speaks to our spirits is through His Word. Study the Bible with diligence, and you will receive spiritual revelation—thoughts that are birthed from God's Spirit to increase your knowledge, understanding, and wisdom.

Hosea 4:6 tells us that God's people are destroyed due to a lack of knowledge. In my early days as a Christian, I had little knowledge of God's Word. I read the Bible, but its words didn't penetrate deep into my soul. In other words, I didn't have revelation. Then I started getting serious about the Bible by taking abundant notes during church services when the Word was preached. I'd take the notes home with me and, all week, I would study what I had learned. If a podcast of the pastor's sermon was available, I would listen to it repeatedly. I finally had focus! I studied one topic and one truth at a time until it was implanted in my heart and started to change me. When I did this, I began to experience the presence and power of God. His Word spoke to me, and it came alive in me!

Having a relationship with God through Jesus Christ is not about religion; it's about intimacy. It's about having a personal connection and communion with our heavenly Father. When you come to know God's Word, you will know God Himself, and you will understand His will. Then, as you live out that will, you will prove that His Word is true and authentic, that it is powerful and gets results. This is because, as you study and receive the truths of the Bible, the Holy Spirit responds by giving you revelation and power.

It's easy to become confused when trying to figure out if God is speaking to us through our hearts, or if what we are hearing within is merely from our own thoughts. The Bible is a wonderful tool for discernment in this regard. If your thoughts line up with Scripture, God is probably speaking to you. Keep reading and studying the Bible. When you become immersed in God's Word, you will learn to recognize and hear the voice of the Lord. (See, for example, John 10:27.)

In earlier chapters of this book, we talked about how vital it is to forgive others in order to receive God's forgiveness ourselves and enter into spiritual and emotional healing. Forgiveness is essential for maintaining a clear relationship with God. When we withhold forgiveness, harbor bitterness, or disobey God's commands in other ways, we create a barrier between ourselves and the Lord. The Bible teaches us that we must not only hear the Word but also obey it. *"But don't just listen to God's word. You must do what it says. Otherwise, you are only fooling yourselves"* (James 1:22 NLT).

God is a loving Father who waits for us to follow His ways. Let us study His Word not merely to gain head knowledge but to understand how to wholeheartedly love and obey the Lord. His commands protect us as they heal our hearts. All of God's Word is good! As 2 Timothy 3:16 says, *"All Scripture is inspired by God and is useful to teach us what is true and to make us realize what is wrong in our lives. It corrects us when we are wrong and teaches us to do what is right"* (NLT).

2. PRAY: SPEAK AND LISTEN

Praying and studying God's Word go hand in hand. They partner together to produce great power within us. When I was a new Christian, I did not understand how to pray. As I grew in my faith, I learned how simple yet life-changing prayer really is. Over the years, many believers have shared with me that their prayer life was stuck or even nonexistent. There are a number of reasons why someone's prayer life might grow cold. It could be that, for various reasons, they no longer hear God's voice as clearly as they used to. Perhaps they have lost the desire to pray. Or, maybe, because of past failures or sins, they feel unworthy of talking to God. Do you identify with any of these scenarios? Always remember that God is ready to hear your prayers and to speak to you when you humbly come to Him in repentance and in search of His truth.

Prayer is communication with God, a conversation in which one party talks and the other listens, and then vice versa. Prayer doesn't have to be complicated. Your prayers don't have to be long, and you don't have to use fancy words. It's as simple as setting aside some quiet time each day, away from the distractions of everyday life. Talk to God as you would talk with a close friend. Tell Him what's going on in your life, what's bothering you, and what you're afraid of. Ask Him for wisdom, help, and revelation.

After you've made your requests known to God, it's time to listen to Him. Use some of your quiet time simply to be still in His presence. Bask in Him. Open yourself up to hearing Him speak to your heart. I believe God regularly speaks to His children. Though He does so in different ways, it's important to know that whatever He says will always line up with Scripture. As I wrote earlier, if your thoughts line up with God's Word, God is likely speaking to you. The number one way we hear from God is through His Word. When you eliminate distractions, enter into your time with the Lord with great expectation, study the Bible, and ask the Holy Spirit to reveal Himself to you and speak to you, He will!

Remember, Jesus taught us that we are to worship God in Spirit and in truth. (See John 4:24.) God is a spiritual Being, which means that we connect with Him through our spirits. There's no magical formula to follow in order to hear from God. He will reveal Himself to you as you regularly seek Him. The more time you spend with Him as you study the Bible and pray, the more you will know Him, and the more you will become familiar with His voice.

God is at work within you every time you spend time with Him! Isn't that amazing? Your spirit is built up, and your connection with Him becomes stronger. He reveals His character to you, the depths of who He is. You get to know His voice and His ways. You learn to trust Him more. You feel empowered as He helps you overcome hardships, trials, and temptations. In time, your prayers become stronger and more articulate. You start praying the words of Scripture, and the words you speak pour out of your heart.

> **GOD IS AT WORK WITHIN YOU EVERY TIME YOU SPEND TIME WITH HIM. YOUR SPIRIT IS BUILT UP, AND YOUR CONNECTION WITH HIM BECOMES STRONGER.**

When you pray, you receive direction, wisdom, and strength to live out the truths and principles in God's Word. I have discovered that many people, after hearing from God, don't follow through with what He has told them to do, which would have led them into their breakthrough or provision. Don't stop short of receiving the healing and other blessings God wants to give you by ignoring the direction He provides you. This is something I had to learn myself. For example, as I described earlier, when Darryl and I were living together before we were married, I knew it was not right. The Lord told me so in my heart a million times, and my disobedience was blocking my relationship with Him. I was literally reading my Bible when the conviction of the Holy Spirit came upon me with such great power. I couldn't take my wrong living any longer. If you remain close to Christ, the Holy Spirit will not allow you to stay in your sin. Conviction produces the desire to get out. The action steps of follow-through are fueled by the courage you summon to do it, even though you are afraid.

I got up from the recliner where I was sitting, walked into the room where Darryl was sleeping, and woke him abruptly. I told him I had something very important to say. He said, "I'm listening." I told him we were not going to have sex anymore. I explained that I was no longer going to compromise but was going to give my everything to Christ. I was going to go after Christ with all that was inside of me. I desired to be fully committed without compromise. The sin, the sleeping together before marriage, had to stop.

I was filled with a grand expectation that Darryl would agree and we would serve the Lord together, without sin. After all, we had been through so much. I had invested my all in believing for this relationship. I had given up everything, for several years, for it to be right. Surely, he would agree. Wrong! He looked right in my eyes and said, "What! I'm out of here!" Through my immediate shock, anger, and heartbreak, I responded, "Yeah, I guess you better. You know, let me help you pack."

When I finally obeyed God's instructions, I grew stronger in my faith. This growth was very painful, but, in the midst of it, I learned to trust God and walk in an upright way. What I thought was a huge loss at the time turned out to be one of my greatest wins! Difficult or painful choices of obedience rarely deliver the instantaneous feelings or results of a victorious win. The victorious outcome begins the moment you make the decision to obey and follow through. The feelings and rewards catch up later. I promise!

In another example, whenever I withheld forgiveness from someone, my prayer life would become dry because my heart was growing stony and cold. I would become easily irritated, experience depression, and have patience for nothing or no one. If we do not follow the direction God gives us, we will become stuck in life. God will not position you for victory if you don't follow His commands. Be quick to obey what you hear from Him.

A life of prayer is developed over time. Don't be discouraged if you have struggled in this area in the past. Just get started or get back on track with a new mindset. Your walk with the Lord will become stronger because, through prayer, you will receive His direction and guidance, just as Proverbs 3:5–6 says: "*Trust in the LORD with all your heart, and lean not on your own understanding; in all your ways acknowledge Him, and He shall direct your paths*" (NKJV).

Prayer is a powerful weapon. When you spend time with God, read His Word, and live out its truths, you will experience great results! You will continue to move out of your pain and experience healing. You will be empowered instead of defeated, encouraged instead of depressed, and enlightened instead of unwise. As you continue to grow spiritually, you will come alive inside and have the courage to move on and move up in God's purposes for you.

3. SPEND TIME WITH FELLOW BELIEVERS

I've previously explained how important it is to become plugged into a local body of believers. Attending a church and getting involved in the life of the congregation is beneficial for many reasons. It gives you the opportunity to connect with, and worship with, other believers; learn about our almighty God and His Word; and be taught to apply God's truths in every area of your life. It also gives you an outlet to give and serve.

Again, going to church doesn't mean just showing up at a weekly Sunday service. It is a time of great power in the presence of the Lord where His Word is taught, revealed, and received! If we do not have the proper perspective regarding church, it becomes a duty we perform instead of a divine encounter with Jesus Himself.

4. SAFEGUARD YOUR LIFE

Ephesians 4:27 tells us not to *"give the devil a foothold"* (NIV). In other words, do not give the enemy any room in your life. Even a little bit of a bad thing is too much. A little conversation with a former romantic partner who isn't following God; a little peek at an inappropriate website; a little drink ("just one won't hurt"); a little dabble of this or a little time with that! "A little" leads right into a fall.

When the enemy is trying to set you up for failure, the Holy Spirit will convict you. You'll get a gut feeling (Holy Spirit conviction) that tells you what you're doing, or are about to do, is wrong. Listen to that feeling that is fighting for your attention. It is the voice of the Lord protecting and leading you away from temptations, heartbreak, painful choices, and, ultimately, destructive consequences. With these warnings, God demonstrates His love for you.

Romans 12:1–2 offers this essential advice for safeguarding our lives:

Therefore, I urge you, brothers and sisters, in view of God's mercy, to offer your bodies as a living sacrifice, holy and pleasing to God—this is your true and proper worship. Do not conform to the pattern of this world, but be transformed by the renewing of your mind. Then you will be able to test and approve what God's will is—his good, pleasing and perfect will. (NIV)

To be holy is to be fully set apart for God. This means we belong to Him, and Him alone. If we have offered our bodies, our habits, our hobbies, our attention, or our focus to unholy people or things, we must realign them with the ways of God. His ways bring healing and protect us from future harm. God is not trying to take away your fun or your freedom. He is trying to lead you into a higher level of living—to significance, purpose, and all the greater things that come from living a life for Him!

Matthew 7:6 says, *"Do not give dogs what is sacred; do not throw your pearls to pigs. If you do, they may trample them under their feet, and turn and tear you to pieces"* (NIV). Earlier, we talked about how it can be necessary to set boundaries in your relationships and lifestyle so you can move forward on your healing journey. To safeguard your life, set some boundaries! Take your power back! You decide who has permission to be in your life and how close to you they are allowed to be. "No" is an anointed word. Say it when it needs to be said. Say what you mean, mean what you say, and say it with confidence. *"Let your 'Yes' be 'Yes,' and your 'No,' 'No'"* (Matthew 5:37 NKJV). Be wise in what you choose to do and who you choose to spend time with.

Now is the time to give serious thought to the people who are in your life, to decide if they are right for you. Protect the mighty work the Holy Spirit is doing within you. Ask yourself these questions as a quick check to help protect your new heart: Do the people I am surrounding myself with love Jesus and demonstrate that love through an active relationship with Him? Is their faith just talk, or do they have a genuine walk with God? Is my own faith strengthened by being around them? Put boundaries on your life to keep from being influenced by people who draw you away from your commitment to Christ, and actively develop close relationships with strong believers who can build you up in the Lord.

You are valuable! You are worthy! You are priceless! You are a son or daughter of the King! Take your rightful place by walking forward in wisdom, confidence, and strength. Live with the right boundaries in place.

> **GOD IS TRYING TO LEAD YOU INTO A HIGHER LEVEL OF LIVING— TO SIGNIFICANCE, PURPOSE, AND ALL THE GREATER THINGS THAT COME FROM LIVING A LIFE FOR HIM.**

5. PROCEED WITH CAUTION

In several places in this book, I've talked about how the Bible teaches us to guard our hearts. *"Guard your heart above all else, for it determines the course of your life"* (Proverbs 4:23 NLT). After you've experienced healing from a traumatic event, a betrayal, a divorce, a spouse's infidelity, stagnation, sorrow, grief, or another difficult situation, it's important to proceed with caution, especially when mending a broken relationship or entering into a relationship with someone new. Allow the power of God and His process of change to prove themselves in your life over time. Be alert, and take things slowly.

I find that most people quickly jump into new relationships or try to rebuild trust too fast with someone who has betrayed them. They give their heart away to people they barely know or disregard their boundaries during the rebuilding process. They base their affections on superficial matters, like looks, status, or what they think is someone's potential, rather than investigating the person's present character or allowing time for that person to reveal their improved character. Remember, any relationship, whether it's a marriage, a dating relationship, a parent-child relationship, a friendship, or a business partnership, requires time to establish or rebuild trust.

The Bible is very clear about the importance of putting trust to the test. Again, allow the true character of a person to be revealed over time before you give your heart away or go full speed ahead. This is especially true when it comes to dating relationships with the goal of marriage in mind. Simply put, be careful not to fall in love with potential or the idea of love you think you can create within the person or the relationship. It is not reality! Don't fall for cheap expressions of affection, physical chemistry, outward excitement, or the promise of financial security. The purpose of dating is to test a person's ability to care for your heart. Let me emphasize again that before you decide if a dating partner would make a good spouse, make sure they are already living out the potential you see in them. Make sure both of you are developing godly character. First things first. You can't expect trustworthy character from someone else if you don't have it yourself.

Time reveals the true character of anyone. Good character goes beyond mere words; it is revealed in a pattern of positive behaviors and actions. A great question to ask yourself to determine someone's trustworthiness is, "Do they do what they say they are going to do?" Be on guard! Look for genuine signs that the other person exhibits strong, stable, godly character. The presence of such character not only establishes trust in a relationship, but it also has the ability to rebuild it after it is broken. Trustworthiness is one of the greatest ways in which genuine love expresses itself.

Why do I focus so much on love and relationships? Because the greatest desire of God's heart is that we commune with Him and have fellowship with other people. As human beings made in God's image, our hearts long to connect with others, and we will relentlessly search for that connection until we find it. But we must proceed with great caution when entering into a love relationship.

Today, there are many ways people can seek relationships, including through online dating services and social media. Let me briefly address online romances based on the trust test. Do you immediately trust every word someone types in their messages when you meet them online? If so, news flash! You don't know who is behind those words. I have counseled many people who hopped on an airplane to marry their online romantic partners the first time they met them in person. Because they fell in love with words, not character, they soon ran into trouble in their relationships.

Online dialogue or texting doesn't create the foundation required to establish trust between people. It's easy to fall in love with someone who doesn't invade your space or test your patience. You shoot an email when you have time or video chat when you look your very best. Relying on chats, email, or texting when establishing a relationship is a setup for heartbreak, friend. Get to know the person—in person and over time. I'm not necessarily knocking relationships that start online. I'm just warning you to proceed with caution. Enter into romantic relationships with the proper perspective.

Similar principles apply in other types of relationships where it's important to proceed with caution. For example, if you're applying for a job, does the company and its leadership have a reputation for integrity and honesty? Do they do the right thing by their customers? If you are considering a business partnership, do you know you can trust the other party to handle their responsibilities and finances well? In your job, do you share every part of your personal life with your coworkers? Be mindful and careful about who you open yourself up to. Guard your heart.

Ask God to send the right people to walk with you in both your personal and professional life.

EMBRACE YOUR HEALING JOURNEY!

Even after our healing takes place, we will still face challenges and difficulties. A Spirit-filled life does not mean a life without hardship and pain. But it does mean we are empowered by God's Spirit to rise above and get through the tough times. It means we are strengthened with the truth that will set us free and *keep* us free.

Because we have gone through the healing process, we now know what to do when wrongs are committed against us because we understand the critical importance of forgiveness. We know that the Lord will work all things for good in our lives as we love and serve Him. We know that, when we live for God through His Spirit, we can overcome all sin, darkness, and defeat. We are able to recognize the lies of the enemy and conquer them because we obey the truth that has been implanted within us through the Word of God.

"Jesus said to the people who believed in him, 'You are truly my disciples if you remain faithful to my teachings. And you will know the truth, and the

truth will set you free.... So if the Son sets you free, you are truly free'" (John 8:31–32, 36 NLT). The great promise of freedom is ours because of Jesus Christ's finished work on the cross, His death, and His resurrection.

Throughout this book, I have described how I wanted to become the woman, mother, daughter, spouse, and friend that God created me to be. I wanted to be powerful and purposeful in His plans for my life. Through God's power and my participation—as I persisted in making courage choices—I am that woman today.

I needed to be well. I needed to be healed so I could be whole. I needed to be repositioned in God's love, in His way of living, and in His process of healing. Everyone I love deserved it, and I deserved it.

And, guess what? You deserve it too. You were made to experience the fullness of God's love, joy, peace, and freedom. As you follow the ways of Jesus, He will perform a miraculous work within you and through you. I thank God for raising us into new life in Christ, with a new heart that can love right and live right. It's time to live well and love well. It's time to be free and to stay free. Embrace your healing journey and awaken to a new life and a future beyond your wildest dreams!

You are worth it, friend!

COURAGE CHOICES FOR YOUR HEALING

1. Which of the five foundational areas are you currently strongest in, and why? Which are you weakest in, and why? Journal your thoughts about how you can actively incorporate each of these principles into your life, especially where you feel you are weakest:

    a. Study God's Word.

    b. Pray: speak *and* listen.

    c. Spend time with fellow believers.

    d. Safeguard your life.

    e. Proceed with caution.

2. In which area of life do you most need healing? Describe how you would like to grow to be purposeful and powerful in God's ways and plans for you.

3. List five power points you pulled from this chapter that will help you safeguard this healing journey you have chosen to embark on, and apply them to your life.

4. What open doors and endless possibilities is God speaking to you about right now? Embrace what He reveals to you! Believe that God will open those doors and provide for those opportunities in His time as you continue to trust and obey Him.

ABOUT THE AUTHOR

Dr. **Tracy Strawberry** is an international speaker, an author, a CEO, and the wife of baseball legend Darryl Strawberry. After many years of battling addiction, alcoholism, dysfunction, and other life-controlling issues, Tracy surrendered her life to Jesus Christ and experienced a radical transformation through the power of God and the process of change. Now she shares her testimony openly as she provides biblical principles and practical solutions for those who are struggling with similar issues.

Tracy is a highly sought-after international speaker, receiving many requests to deliver her powerful messages on how to see lasting change, reinvent yourself, experience God in the most difficult of times, overcome your past, and become the very best "you" that God created you to be. She has a doctorate in theology with a focus on cultural restoration and leadership, a master's degree in business administration and management, and a bachelor's degree in ministry leadership. She is the author of several publications, including *Imperfect Marriage: Help for Those Who Think It's Over* (with Darryl Strawberry) and *Clean, Sober & Saved*, a Christ-centered recovery curriculum that is used globally.

In her weekly programs and traveling ministry, Tracy delivers a message of faith, redeeming hope, restoration, and freedom in Jesus Christ. She believes that those who are lost will be found and those who are bound will be free! In addition to her biblical teaching and preaching platform, Tracy is an international business consultant with a specialty in assisting pastors, governmental officials, and other leaders with infrastructure and organizational development, strategic planning, and the creation of innovative solutions for reaching culturally diverse demographics and territories.

Welcome to Our House!

We Have a Special Gift for You

It is our privilege and pleasure to share in your love of Christian books. We are committed to bringing you authors and books that feed, challenge, and enrich your faith.

To show our appreciation, we invite you to sign up to receive a specially selected **Reader Appreciation Gift**, with our compliments. Just go to the Web address at the bottom of this page.

God bless you as you seek a deeper walk with Him!

WE HAVE A GIFT FOR YOU. VISIT:

whpub.me/nonfictionthx

WHITAKER HOUSE